Chipotle

Chile Cook Book

JACQUELINE HIGUERA MCMAHAN

The Olive Press

BOOK DESIGN :RUTH HIGHTOWER
PHOTOGRAPHY :ROBERT MCMAHAN

Published by Olive Press
P.O. Box 194, Lake Hughes, CA 93532

Library of Congress Catalogue Number 94-069177
ISBN: 1-881656-03-9

Printed and bound in the United States of America

TO LIZ,
WHO IS NOW APPRECIATING CHIPOTLES
FROM SOME DISTANT PLACE

OTHER BOOKS BY JACQUELINE HIGUERA MCMAHAN
CALIFORNIA RANCHO COOKING,1983
THE SALSA BOOK, 1986
THE RED AND GREEN CHILE BOOK, 1988
THE HEALTHY FIESTA, 1990
THE MEXICAN BREAKFAST BOOK, 1992
THE HEALTHY MEXICAN COOKBOOK, 1994

And so they did not tarry. They rested overnight and in the morning the column set out, marching briskly along a causeway toward the end of the rainbow.

William Weber Johnson

Led by Cortés,
the Spanish conquistadores approached
the great Aztec capital, Tenochtitlan,
from the rich and elegant lesser city of Ixtapalapa.

They were fearful
and yet spurred on by the hope for boundless riches.

Little did they know
how ephemeral the promise of gold would be
and how the foods of this New World
would outlast the gold they would find.

Our appetite for chiles and our old love of chocolate,
both treasures of the Aztec world
are testimony to this.

ACKNOWLEDGEMENTS

I am very grateful to my family for following a steady diet of chipotles during the course of this book (now they're hopelessly addicted), to the number of chile experts and chile growers who have patiently answered questions about chipotles and the art of smoking. It was as though we were trying to forge a trail into the age-old preservation of chiles first practiced by ancient cultures. Many, many of my questions have been answered. My thanks go to:

THE AZTECS, for starting it all.

MY HUSBAND, ROBERT, for letting me find him in Mexico during the fireworks of diez y seis de septiembre so we could share chiles all of these years.

MY GRANDMOTHER, for giving me red chile at an early age in the form of red enchiladas for breakfast accompanied by coffee laced with Pet milk and all the sugar I wanted.

MY SONS, IAN AND O'REILLY for eating chiles while I raised them to manhood and who thought at one time that I even put chipotles into cake (I did).

LEE AND WAYNE JAMES and EVIE TRUXAW for sharing chile knowledge, for pursuing the art of smoking chiles to perfection, and having adventursome spirits.

JOSE MARMOLEJO, for being a friend and answering all of my questions so expertly.

STUART HUDSON, for growing such delicious chiles along the Rio Grande and sharing knowledge about growing and smoking chiles.

JEAN ANDREWS, whose beautiful book, *Peppers*, is such a resource and who is generous with her knowledge.

CHEFS such as Michele Anna Jordan of the Jaded Palate in Sonoma, Eric Tucker of Milly's in San Rafael, Alex Diaz of Chileto's of Santa Barbara, Roger Hayot of the Authentic Cafe in Los Angeles for letting me borrow from their chipotle recipes; as well as W. Park Kerr who suggested I steal all or part of one of his recipes.

RUTH HIGHTOWER, who I think learned to love chipotles while she was editing and designing this book.

Contents

INTRODUCTION

CHAPTER II

CHAPTER IV

Chipotle Chiles
The Thousand Year Old Cooking Secret

During the fifteen-year period that has passed since I first discovered chipotles, I have gone over the edge. I cannot think of another ingredient that has seduced me to this great a degree. If olive oil has a taste as old as water, the chipotle chile has a fragrance as old and elusive as smoke.

When the conquistadores set foot in ancient Tenochtitlan, chipotles were in the city's marketplaces. In the Aztec language of Nahuatl, "chil" refers to chile and "pochilli" to smoke. The shortened word, chipotle, means simply smoked chile.

The inventive Aztecs devised smoking techniques to dry and preserve thick-walled chiles such as the jalapeños which are difficult to dry in humid climates. The smoked chiles became a prized cooking ingredient and the technique an art in itself, an art surrounded by mystery.

In my own quest for answers, my questions often evolved into more questions, but I have come away with a reward—an ingredient as delicious as it is mysterious.

The chipotle's presence in a dish makes it seem as though ten different spices have been added, a great accomplishment for a little chile that reaches back in time to an Aztec smoke pit.

I hope that the pages of this book become imbued with the fragrance of chipotle smoke as you turn to discover new recipes.

CHAPTER I

*C*HIPOTLES, *FIRE WITH FLAVOR*

..., all smoked chiles are chipotles with flavors varying as widespread as Mexico's regions from Chihuahua to Yucatan. What you get when you cook with chipotle chiles is a concentrated flavor mingled with concentrated fire with concentrated intensities of smoke. It is this evolution of flavor, fire, and smoke into one little chile that makes chipotles one of the best cooking secrets to hit the kitchen.

Definitive Qualities of Chipotles, What to Look For

Even in Mexico there are variations in chipotle nomenclature derived from the region the chiles were grown, who smoked them, and who named them. Sometimes everyone in a village calls them mecos and

everyone in the next village c[...]
moras.

Rather than worry too much [...]
names, base your judgment of [...]
the following qualities:

Flavor. You want a rich chile [...]
spicy and chocolaty overton[...]
chipotles have a bright berr[...]
the moritas and some have [...]
with a hint of sweetness or [...]

Smokiness. Greatly affects flavor. Will vary
depending upon what was used to smoke
the chiles which could be anything from
mesquite, pecan, fruitwood, grapevine
cuttings, palmetto, or some wood indig-
enous to a particular area of Mexico or
even old truck tires (just kidding).

Heat. Heat is the fire that chipotle-heads live
and die for. Chile heat has a broad scale.
Smoked chiles tend to be hotter than their
fresh counterparts. There are two theories
explaining this phenomenon: when you
dehydrate chiles by smoke-drying, the
percentage of capsaicin (chile oil) becomes
greater in relationship to the chile itself.
Smoked chiles are dried to less than half

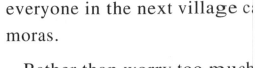

their size when plump and fresh; also, the heat of smoking encourages the penetration of capsaicin into the chile flesh. When you finish eating a dish spiced with chipotles, your mouth will feel the heat in the front around your lips which some say is what makes the chipotle high more sensual.

Smoked Chiles Available in the United States

⟨ **Chipotles***:* whitish tan color because they are smoked when green instead of when red; about 3 inches long. Their taste is more smoke and heat than fruit. Often found in cellophane packets in Mexican markets. These chipotles are the most widely distributed in the United States. Try to find them when they are still pliable as they can be quite leathery and need a good soaking in hot water.

⟨ **Morita chiles:** deep burnished red with a flavor of smoke and berries; lightly smoked ripe serrano chiles or jalapeño type. Grown in central Mexico; often available through chile vendors in the United States. Sometimes just called chipotle.

⟨ **Mora chiles:** deep burnished red with a flavor of smoke and plums. Not as hot as moritas. They should have a rounded tip as they are most often a jalapeño type. Mora means blackberry or mulberry. From northern Mexico, may be referred to as chipotles. Available more frequently from chile vendors rather than in markets in the U.S.A.. (See Resources for shipping information.)

⟨ **Chile pasado ahumado:** red New Mexican chiles that have been roasted, skinned, and slow smoke-dried for flavor; have bright, hot smoky flavor and reconstitute immediately when added to hot dishes making them perfect for quesadillas. Available through Rancho Mesilla, New Mexico. (See Resources for shipping information.)

⟨ **Freshly-smoked chipotles:** can be any one of jalapeño type like tam jalapeño (mildly hot) or mitla jalapeño (very hot); have a caramelized smoky cherry heat that is irresistible; their intense smokiness can vary depending upon whether a particular batch was smoked with prunewood, applewood, or grapevine cuttings; available at Marin Farmer's Market or Tierra

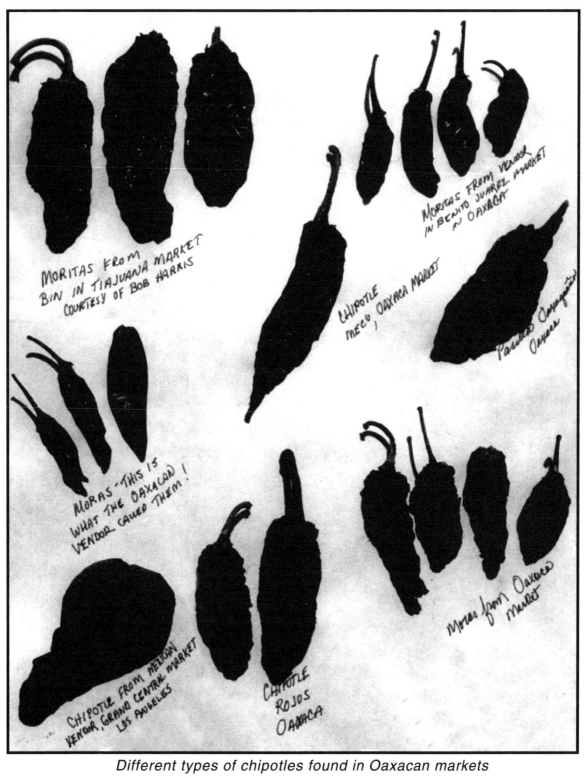

MORITAS FROM
BIN IN TIAJUANA MARKET
COURTESY OF BOB HARRIS

MORITAS FROM VENDOR
IN BENITO JUAREZ MARKET
IN OAXACA

CHIPOTLE
MECO, OAXACA MARKET

PASILLA OAXAQUEÑO
OAXACA

MORAS - THIS IS
WHAT THE OAXACAN
VENDOR CALLED THEM!

MORAS FROM OAXACA
MARKET

CHIPOTLE FROM MEXICAN
VENDOR, GRAND CENTRAL MARKET
LOS ANGELES

CHIPOTLE
ROJOS
OAXACA

Different types of chipotles found in Oaxacan markets

Vegetable Farm, Healdsburg, CA. (See Resources for shipping information.)

Smoked Chiles Available in Regions of Mexico

The Mexican smoked chiles mentioned above—the chipotles, moritas, and mora chiles—are those most commonly shipped to vendors in the United States. There are other smoked chiles that can be found only in Mexican marketplaces in the Districto Federal, Veracruz, Puebla, Oaxaca, and Chiapas in particular. Listed below are some of the common names of smoked chiles found in the markets:

⟨ **Meco:** another term for a type of jalapeño, meco refers to the color of blackish red. Resembles the mora.

⟨ **Pasilla oaxaqueño:** found in the market-places of Oaxaca; a chile slightly larger than jalapeño; used in moles, salsas, and in the regional dish, pasillas rellenos (stuffed chiles).

⟨ **Moritas:** smaller, more triangular shaped moritas found in southern Mexico, like in the Oaxacan markets; a burnished dark

Remember:
*The generic term for all smoked chiles is **chipotle**, but not all smoked chiles are chipotles. Here are the other names they go by.*

red chile whose size can vary depending upon the region in Mexico where it is grown; can be as small as serrano and as large as a jalapeño.

⟨ **Huauchinango:** a huge jalapeño not to be confused with the Veracruzano fish, huachinango.

⟨ **Moras:** mora refers to the blackberry color of the ripe chile, a jalapeño type whose size and shape can vary depending upon the region where it is grown.

The Mystery of Smoking Chipotles in Mexico

As chipotles have gained in popularity, more interest has been generated in how the smoking is done. It is as though a secret society of artisans is sheltering the craft with mystery.

Information is getting out when knowledgeable people make trips into chile-growing areas. Through the persistent questioning and observations of chile experts such as Jose Marmolejo of the Austin-based Don Alfonso Foods, we have learned that there are traveling chile men who go from farm to farm to smoke the chile crops as they are harvested. A large farm might have a smoker built on the edge of the chile fields. The ripe, red chiles at the end of the growing season are carried from field to smoker. The smoker has a 3 foot high base of stones with wire-mesh racks to hold the chiles away from the heat. For about ten hours, the men move and rake the chiles around on the racks using long sticks to prevent the chiles from burning over any hot spots above the smoldering embers. After this initial smoking, the chiles are left in the hot sun to complete their drying.

A couple of years ago Dr. Paul Bosland known as Dr. Chile, of the Agronomy and Horticulture Department of New Mexico State University, went on a fact-finding mission to Delicos, Mexico where many chipotles are processed. He reported another smoking method: a deep underground pit to contain the smoldering fires. Small tunnels lead to a rack, holding the chiles, where drafts of air pull the smoke up over the chiles.

Searching for Chipotle Mecca

Wayne James, part of the sister-brother team that operates Tierra Vegetable Farm in

Healdsburg, California, became so determined to find out how Mexican farmers smoked their chiles he went to Oaxaca with his friend Evie Truxaw who is bilingual. For days they wandered through marketplaces asking questions. They were told that Puebla was the center of commercial chipotle production, but this didn't interest them since they really wanted to witness smoking the old-fashioned way, not a factory system.

Finally they encountered an old man selling the pasilla oaxaqueñas and his own homemade chipotle paste outside the Abastos market. He told them that his chiles came from the mountains. The city of Oaxaca is surrounded by mountains but they were pointed in the direction of Zacatepec. When Wayne and Evie discovered it was a seven hour journey on a second class bus, they opted to rent a Volkswagen which took them over dirt roads with hair-raising proximity to the edges of cliffs. They drove past waterfalls spilling onto the road and gave rides to a couple of men trudging up the mountain. The men assured them at a fork in the road that Zacatepec, where they were headed, was the village of chipotles.

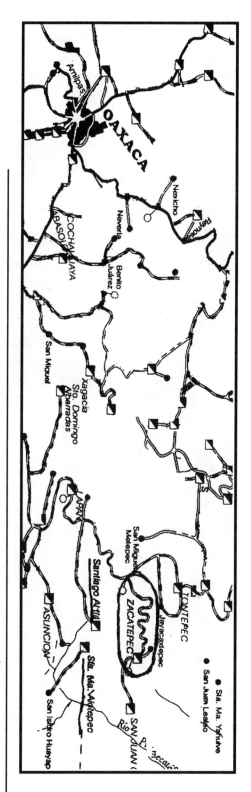

Grandma's refrigerator, used for smoking chiles!

Three hours after the fork, they arrived in Zacatepec, a village nestled just above the clouds. They expected to see smokers now that they had arrived in Mecca. Asking more questions, they were guided to the village mescal parlor where three slightly pickled men took them to a house where four generations of their family were spellbound before a television. "Where are the chipotles," Evie queried. "Oh, we don't do that here," the television watchers responded.

No one in Zacatepec was smoking chipotles. Wrong village, wrong month. It was December and harvesting was done. The village where the chiles are smoked is just a few cloud levels down to a warmer valley but only reachable by foot. Evie and Wayne did find out that many chile farmers smoke chipotles over a grill of green twigs placed over barely smoldering fires set in the fields. The advice given repeatedly was, "No flames." The real flavor comes from slow, slow smoking over smoldering embers.

Wayne and Evie had to face the trip down the mountain in the rented Volkswagen before dark and were out of time. They had driven about 200 kilometers to find the secret to Mexican chipotles and arrived back in Oaxaca with just a great story and the adventure behind them. The mystery continues. They have vowed to make a return trip so that they may hike into Santiago Atitla and Alotepec, the two villages that make chipotles. So it has been said.

Meanwhile, after much more research Wayne constructed an elaborate chile smoker out of brick and block. In an outside fire pit, dry fuel is used to start the fire which is then fed with the farm's own green applewood, prunewood, cherrywood, and grapevine trimmings to create the flavorful smoke. The smoke is then piped to the smoker. The fruitwood is what gives an added dimension to the Tierra Vegetable chipotles which rank as extraordinary in the realm of smoked chiles.

Once the brick of Wayne's smoker heats up, the draw is better than the previous smoker, Grandma's vintage 1950 refrigerator, used in last year's initial experiments. The heat and smoke are better distributed so the chiles don't bake or burn before they are smoked. The James' can now smoke 200 pounds of chiles at a time in the brick

Wayne James' newly built chile smoker, Healdsburg, California

Advice for smoking chiles:
"No Flames!"
"¡No Fuego!"

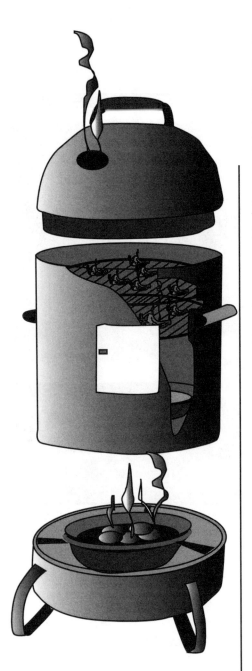

smoker. This is definitely an intensive operation since it takes 15 to 20 pounds of fresh chiles to make 1 pound of chipotles. But then again 1 pound of chipotles goes a long way.

After freezing an overabundance of ripe jalapeños, Lee and Wayne tried smoking the frozen chiles which collapsed more in the smoker than the fresh chiles, releasing more surface sugar encouraging caramelization. These caramelized chipotles are a favorite of many San Francisco Bay Area chefs.

Home Smoking

After absorbing the information garnered from different friends and helpful chile experts, I began wondering if chile smoking was possible on a very small scale. Could I do it? During one of the hottest summers in years, the jalapeño and fresno chiles wereturning red early in the season, just asking to be smoked. I had to try the rite of smoking chipotles for myself and probe the mystery, not being able to make a quick trip to Santiago Atitla in the near future.

Perfect Chiles for Smoking

Use ripe, red chiles that are available usually from midsummer to autumn. Because of their ripe state, red chiles are richer in flavor with more sweetness just as ripe fruit is sweeter than green. If the chiles are a little wrinkled, that's fine, they have just begun to lose moisture; but do not use chiles that show signs of mold or have soft spots that may indicate rot.

I found a slightly dented Char-Broil meat smoker on sale at a hardware store and snapped it up. We had great success on our first attempt at home smoking chipotles:

1) First build a base fire of hardwood briquettes, using an electric starter or starter sticks. When the coals are hot but covered by white ash, you can add the smoking material.

2) Add small pieces (we used 4 inch chunks) of fruitwood, almond or pecan wood which you have had soaking in a bucket of water for a couple of hours.

3) Add water-soaked hickory chips. You want to keep a balance between having a smoldering fire, not so hot that it burns the

Note:

Try to maintain a heat between 150°–175°. Check heat using an oven thermometer placed on rack with chiles.

Red jalapeño and fresno chiles placed on rack for smoking

chiles, and not adding so much soaked wood and chips that you put the fire out. Add soaked wood chunks and chips every 30 minutes. If you have pieces of green fruitwood, such as they use at Tierra Vegetable Farm, that is the best smoking fuel.

If you have to leave or go to bed, just allow the smoker to go out. When you return or get up you can start the smoldering fires again if the chiles aren't smoked enough.

The Char-Broil smoker has a basin for water which we ignored during our first try. We have found that it helps to add a couple of inches of water to the basin because it helps disperse the heat. The smoker racks are several inches above the water basin. We place about 2 pounds of ripe chiles on each rack. Heat is drawn up the edges of the smoker causing hot spots around the edges of the rack; the chiles placed here can toast so it is necessary to move them around the racks and toward the center. This is a good job to do every time you replenish fire.

Fire in base of smoker, started with charcoal.

Turn chiles over so they smoke evenly.

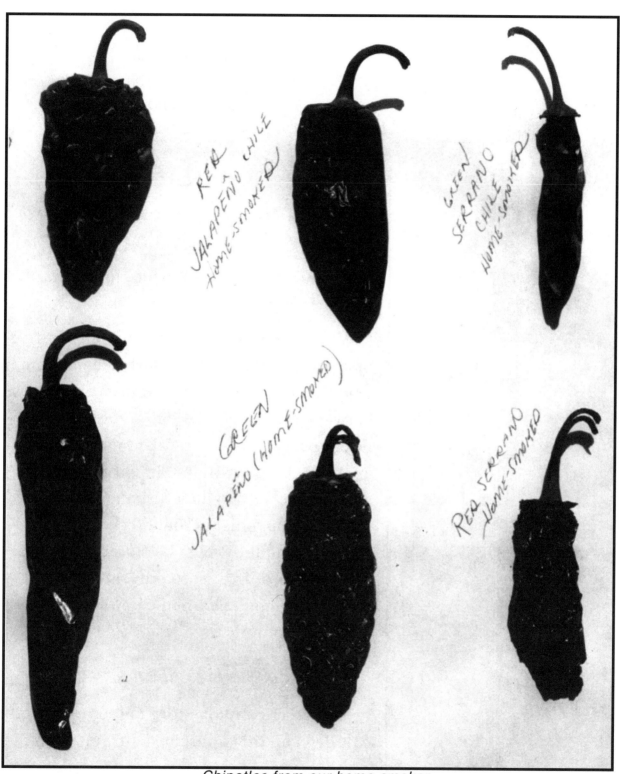

RED JALAPEÑO CHILE HOME-SMOKED

GREEN SERRANO CHILE HOME-SMOKED

GREEN JALAPEÑO (HOME-SMOKED)

RED SERRANO HOME-SMOKED

Chipotles from our home smoker.

Smoking Time—How Long is Long Enough?

Home-smoking chiles takes about 10 to 12 hours, making it a perfect job to start in the early morning.

When are chiles smoked enough? In five or six hours, they have absorbed a maximum amount of smoke flavor and they have lost between 60 and 90 percent of their moisture. I personally do not like them when they are bone dry dehydrated. In our home smoker, we tend to underdry them because we like them moist (about 50 percent dehydration). But they must be stored in the refrigerator or freezer to prevent any mold whereas completely dried chipotles can be stored for months.

Storing Chipotles

How long can you store chipotles? Typical, dry chipotles purchased from a chile vendor, Mexican store, or Mexican market-place can be kept for months. Fresher chipotles, such as the ones cured at Tierra Vegetable Farm should be stored in the freezer, tightly sealed in a Ziploc bag. In fact, I recommend that all dried chiles, except decorative ristras, be stored in the freezer due to their susceptibility to insects. Chiles draw bugs like honey draws bees. Bugs know what is good.

When I plan on using freshly smoked chiles immediately, I smoke jalapeños for just 4 hours and then chop them for a salsa fresca. The chiles are still soft but lazily smoky, making a great-tasting salsa.

How to Cook with Chipotles

Dried chipotles

These are the favorite of the chipotle aficionados who want fire, smoke, and that fruity heat found especially in dried chipotles. You will find them in Mexican stores and well-stocked ethnic sections of large supermarkets. Vegetable departments in supermarkets can order them from suppliers like Frieda's Gourmet Produce in Los Angeles. I have had them arrive by the next day. You can order chiles directly from chile suppliers such as Don Alfonso Foods which is as close to you as your phone and handy plastic card.

Which dried chipotle will you need? If you are like me, you will base your decision on availability or how fast you can get them by phone and which chile tastes best to you. Many chefs prefer the bright flavor of the lightly smoked moritas. The whitish tan, ugly chipotles are commercially smoked, but they are the chipotles that I started with over fifteen years ago so I do have to be somewhat loyal. If you need a smoky hot flavor they will give it to you.

Reconstituting dried chipotles

Most of the time, before using dried chiles in a recipe, you have to soak them. Reconstitute by pouring boiling water over the chiles and soaking for 20 to 45 minutes. If the chiles are really dry, they will require the longer time. If the chiles are soft and pliable, they may be ready after 20 minutes of soaking. When I use the freshly smoked chipotles from Tierra Vegetables, they are ready after 5 minutes of soaking.

Chipotle paste

After the chiles have soaked, place them in a blender with a little of the soaking liquid. For 6 soaked chipotles, use about 2 tablespoons of soaking liquid. You can make up a batch of chipotle paste and store it in a glass jar in the refrigerator for a couple of weeks. For more complex flavor, make a seasoned Chipotle Paste by blending the pureed chipotles with

    1 tablespoon olive oil,
    2 cloves garlic,
    the juice of 1 lime or
      1 tablespoon of white wine vinegar,
    1/2 teaspoon salt.

Quick chipotle mayonnaise

Stir 2 tablespoons of the above seasoned Chipotle Paste into 3/4 cup regular or reduced-fat mayonnaise. Use for sandwiches, tortas, or for dipping artichoke leaves. You can also combine the seasoned Chipotle Paste with sour cream or yogurt; or use half reduced-fat mayonnaise and half nonfat yogurt blended with 2 tablespoons of seasoned Chipotle Paste for a delicious lower calorie spread for sandwiches.

Chipotle powder

Another way to treat dried chipotles is to pulverize them in an old electric coffee grinder (that you don't use for coffee anymore!). You don't have to soak the chipotles in hot water. This treatment works especially well with very dry chiles. Sprinkle the chipotle powder into sauces, soups, and stews just as you would regular chile powder. Go easy with amounts as the powder is quite potent.

Chipotles en Adobo (Chipotles Adobado)

These chipotles are easy to love and easy to use and they are my recommendation for first time chipotle cooks. Chipotles en adobo are found in 7-ounce cans, pickled in a chile-based sauce. Depending upon the brand you buy, some are more vinegary and some are in more of a tomato sauce, my least favorite. Herdez is a good brand. Look in the ethnic sections of large supermarkets or in Mexican stores. Don Alfonso Foods make some of the best chipotles en adobo canned in jars (See Resources). Their flavorful sauce of ancho chiles and herbs makes these chipotles very suave. You can easily put a scoop of

pureed chipotles en adobo into soups, stews, and sauces. This is definitely the handiest way to use chipotles although the flavor of smoke is less pronounced.

Making Your Own Chipotles en Adobo

If you have purchased a large batch of chipotles (moras or moritas) and would like to preserve them, this is a way to do it. Eric Tucker, the chef at Milly's in San Rafael, just throws a bunch of chipotles into his stock ancho chile sauce and simmers them for 1 to 2 hours. This is one of those advantages of having big pots of sauce and stock simmering all the time.

Below is the easy way for those of us who are home cooks.

Homemade Chipotles en Adobo

Pour the boiling water over the chipotles and ancho chiles. Soak for 30 minutes. Remove all the chile stems but leave the seeds. In a blender, puree 6 of the soaked chipotles, ancho chiles, the tomatoes, and 1 cup of the soaking liquid.

Place the puree in a 3-quart heavy pot

HOMEMADE CHIPOTLES EN ADOBO

1/4 pound chipotles, moras, moritas, or home-smoked chiles

4 ancho chiles

2 quarts boiling water for soaking

2 large tomatoes, broiled or charred over flame

1 head garlic, top sliced off

2 bay leaves

1 teaspoon cumin seeds, mashed

1 teaspoon oregano

1 stick canela or cinnamon

3 cloves, crushed

1 sprig thyme

1/2 cup apple cider vinegar

1-1/2 cups water

1 tablespoon olive oil

1 tablespoon brown sugar

1 and 1/2 teaspoons salt

with the rest of the ingredients: the remaining soaked moritas, garlic, bay leaves, mashed cumin seeds, oregano, cinnamon, cloves, thyme, vinegar, water, olive oil, brown sugar, and salt.

Simmer for 45 minutes until flavors blend and chiles become unctuously soft. Store in a glass quart jar in the refrigerator for up to 2 months. The adobo sauce will thicken as it sits.

Use just the adobo sauce as a delicious addition for a lighter chipotle flavoring. You can also puree the entire batch of chipotles and the adobo sauce to make it even easier to add to recipes. Before pureeing chipotles, remove cinnamon and whole bay leaves.

CHAPTER II

CREATIONS WITH CHIPOTLES

When I first discovered chipotles, it was within the dark labyrinth of the old, unrestored Grand Central Market on 3rd and Hill in Los Angeles. The leathery-looking dried chiles had an overpowering smokiness that heated up the nostrils at first whiff.

I brought a half-dozen home to try. I didn't buy enough. On first try, I used the chipotle with great caution which was soon thrown to the wind. More and more I began looking for excuses to include them in new ways—like stuffing them under the skin of an unsuspecting turkey breast before roasting. A boon to my own imagination has been the imagination of various chefs who were also discovering intoxicating ways with chipotles. I have borrowed from their ideas and creativity and am now greatly indebted.

I hope you aren't assuming that I put chipotles in everything (well, while working on this book they were included in our steady diet). I don't. I want the chipotle to shine, so it has to be juxtaposed next to things that complement and mellow its flavors. A fiery chipotle-dressed salad goes well with barbecued chicken. While testing recipes for this book, a typical dinner included three chipotle dishes. I do not recommend this menu for most people although I can think of a few. But if there happened to be a day when I served nothing with chipotle, we ate in stunned silence, wondering why the meal seemed, well, missing something.

If there is something such as chipotle overload, I cannot testify in its behalf. A day without chipotle is like a day without sunshine. The recipes included here are my favorites. Buen provecho!

Note
When a recipe calls for a chipotle, you can use other smoked chiles such as a mora, morita, or freshly smoked chile.

CHIPOTLE CHILES LOVE

HONEY

LIME, LEMON, AND ORANGE JUICE

CINNAMON

TROPICAL FRUITS

BARBECUE SAUCE

SEAFOOD

PORK

CHICKEN

CREAM

SOUR CREAM

MAYONNAISE

You can combine chipotle chiles with any of the above ingredients and they will complement the flavors.

Barbecued Turkey Breast with Chipotles and Thyme
Serves 6 with leftovers for sandwiches

During the heat of summer while I was working on this book, I prepared this recipe many times. It is really easy, the work is done outside on the barbecue so the kitchen doesn't get hot, and we love slices of this spicy turkey for sandwiches and salads in the dog days that follow. This means no cooking for at least a couple of days!

While the chipotles are soaking, prepare the turkey. Use your fingers to loosen the skin without breaking through it. Try to leave the skin attached to the outer edges of the breast so you can stuff in more chipotles without risk of them falling out. The attached skin at the edge will hold them in.

Rub the olive oil and seasoning salt under the skin over the breast. Press the chipotles under the skin also, over the entire breast. If you want more heat, use a scissors to open up the chipotles. Lay them flat. After the chipotles are well-packed under the skin, place in the sprigs of thyme. Press the tur-

BARBECUED TURKEY BREAST

WITH CHIPOTLES AND THYME

10 chipotle chiles, soaked in
hot water until pliable

One 2 to 3 pound whole turkey
breast

1 tablespoon olive oil

1 tablespoon seasoning salt

4 long sprigs of fresh thyme

key skin down. Rub the outside with a little olive oil and more seasoning salt.

Place the turkey breast, bone side down, over a low fire. I have used a gas barbecue for this very successfully. If possible, keep the cover down on the barbecue to increase the smoking. After 30 minutes, turn the turkey over and grill on the other side for 20 minutes. Watch carefully so it doesn't grill too quickly. Turn breast back to bone side for about another 20 minutes. The exact timing will depend on size of the turkey breast and heat of your barbecue. It is best to check using a meat thermometer. Cook to about 170°. Let turkey rest at least 15 minutes before slicing.

Rustic Chipotle Mashed Potatoes
Serves 4 to 6 as a side

These potatoes are called rustic because some of the peel is purposely left on. If you do this with regular mashed potatoes they turn grayish tan, but with Chipotle Mashed Potatoes it seems a natural thing to do. The earthiness of the potato skins goes with chipotle.

Serve these potatoes with simple roasted chicken and a salad. Or surprise everyone for the holidays.

Place head of garlic on a square of foil. Rub top of garlic with olive oil and cover with sprig of thyme. Fold edges of foil over garlic, making a little packet. Roast in pre-heated 375° oven (or toaster oven) for 45 minutes.

Meanwhile, remove some of peel off potatoes in strips; the potato should look striped. Cut potatoes in thirds and place in salted boiling water. Boil over medium heat for about 25 minutes. When you can easily pierce potato with a thin knife, they are done.

RUSTIC CHIPOTLE MASHED POTATOES

1 head garlic, top sliced off

1 teaspoon olive oil

1 sprig thyme or oregano

4 Idaho potatoes

2 teaspoons salt for cooking water

Place potatoes in bowl of heavy-duty mixer or mash with potato masher. Pierce each clove of soft, roasted garlic with the tip of a paring knife to remove easily. In the bowl with the boiled potatoes, place 8 cloves roasted garlic, butter, sour cream, warm milk, chipotle, and cheese. Whip the potatoes with the flat blade of the mixer or just mash everything together. Add salt to taste. Place potatoes in a serving bowl and sprinkle top with red chile.

Suggestion!
When I don't have chipotles on hand, I just add 2 tablespoons of ground New Mexican chile powder to the mashed potatoes.

3 tablespoons butter

1/4 cup sour cream

About 1/2 cup warm milk

2 tablespoons pureed chipotle en adobo

1/2 cup sharp white Cheddar cheese

Salt to taste

1 teaspoon ground red chile for garnish

Riso Pasta Salad With Corn and Black Beans, Chipotle Lime Dressing
Serves 6

For this particular dish I like to use a good brand of chipotles en adobo like Don Alfonso's whose chipotles en adobo are in a great tasting sauce using ancho chiles that provide more added flavor.
Puree chipotles and some of their adobo sauce in blender.

RISO PASTA SALAD WITH CORN

AND BLACK BEANS,

CHIPOTLE LIME DRESSING

Boiling water

2 teaspoons salt

1-1/2 cups riso pasta (rice-shaped pasta)

1/4 cup balsamic vinegar

1/4 cup lime juice

2 tablespoons olive oil

1 teaspoon minced garlic

Years ago when I took a cooking class with Paul Prudhomme in New Orleans, he gave a marvelous recipe for Cajun Potato Salad and then cautioned, "Never serve potato salad cold, it ruins it." He felt that once a potato salad had been chilled in an ice box, it never tasted as good as when you first stirred it together. I feel the same way about pasta salad. I really don't like those cold, congealed, flavorless pasta salads in deli display cases. This riso pasta salad is best when you stir it together and serve it warm although the rice-shaped riso pasta (sometimes called orzo) is one of the pastas that doesn't get starchy and congealed after it's been chilled.

Bring 4 quarts water to a boil. Add salt. Stir in pasta and keep on medium heat. Stir frequently so it doesn't clump. Cook for 10 minutes. Test to see if pasta is tender. Pour into colander. Rinse with cold water.

While pasta is cooking, stir together the marinade of balsamic vinegar, lime juice, olive oil, and minced garlic. Pour this marinade over the warm riso once it has been drained and lightly rinsed.

Prepare your diced red onions. I like to use the frozen tiny corn niblets and cook them just until they are no longer icy. Or cook 2 ears of fresh corn for just a couple of minutes and cut off the kernels with a sharp knife. You can use canned black beans or your own cooked black beans. I often cook a big pot of black beans and freeze small amounts in yogurt containers just for occasions like this. Canned beans work in a pinch but they are softer and saltier.

Stir olive oil, lime juice, mayonnaise, and chipotle puree together. Add the red onions, corn, and black beans to the marinated riso. Stir the chipotle mayonnaise into the mixture. Lastly add the cilantro. Taste for seasoning and add salt and pepper if needed. You can add more chipotle puree if you really need the heat but don't overpower the other flavors! Puree chipotles and some of their adobo sauce in the blender.

1 cup diced red onion

1/2 cup cooked corn kernels

1 cup cooked but firm black beans, rinsed in strainer

2 teaspoons olive oil

1 tablespoon lime juice

2 tablespoons mayonnaise, regular or reduced fat

1 tablespoon chipotle puree (see recipe note)

1/2 cup snipped cilantro

Salt and freshly ground black pepper to taste

Chipotles curing in a home smoker.

GRILLED SWORDFISH OR

SHARK TACOS

1/4 cup lime juice

1 tablespoon olive oil

2 teaspoons minced garlic

1 chipotle chile en adobo

2 teaspoons adobo liquid

1-1/2 pounds swordfish or
*   shark steaks*

1/2 cup chopped onion,
*   preferably red*

1/4 cup snipped cilantro

12 corn tortillas, warmed

Garnishes:

Fresh Pineapple Salsa (recipe
*   page 122)*

2 cups chopped romaine lettuce

1 cup thinly sliced cabbage

Grilled Swordfish or Shark Tacos
Serves 4

A million light years away from grease-laden tacos, these fish tacos were inspired by the boatmen off the Yucatan Peninsula who once served me one of the best picnics I ever ate: freshly caught fish grilled over palmetto on a Caribbean beach. These tacos are superb with Fresh Pineapple Salsa. See page 122

Blend together the lime juice, olive oil, garlic, chipotle chile, and adobo liquid. Rub mixture all over the fish. Let marinate at least 20 minutes at room temperature.

Grill fish over hot coals covered with white ash, until it just barely flakes, about 10 minutes per side for thick steaks. Do not overcook as you want the fish to remain moist. Remove fish to a plate and cut into chunks. Add the chopped onion and cilantro.

Warm the tortillas on a griddle or nonstick pan or wrap in foil and bake for 10 minutes. To serve, each person spoons some of the fish mixture into a warm tortilla and adds salsa, lettuce, and cabbage as desired.

Marilyn's Chipotle Shrimp in Tequila
Serves 4

Marilyn Harryman helped me search for chipotles five years ago in San Francisco's Hispanic neighborhood, known by the natives simply as the Mission. This is another simple recipe that Marilyn stirs up in under ten minutes. You can also wrap these shrimp up in warm corn tortillas for soft tacos, or serve shrimp over pasta.

Heat olive oil in a large (12-inch) non-stick skillet and sauté shrimp over high flame in two batches, just until they turn pink. This will take about 3 minutes since the shrimp is frozen.

Put all the shrimp in the skillet with the garlic, chipotle, lime, tequila and salt to taste. Simmer for a minute on high heat to reduce liquid. Tip pan toward flame of burner so the tequila flames and burns off. Stir in cilantro and salt. Serve shrimp over rice or pasta.

MARILYN'S CHIPOTLE

SHRIMP IN TEQUILA

3 teaspoons virgin olive oil

1 pound of large frozen shrimp

1 tablespoon minced garlic

2 teaspoons ground
  chipotles or 2 freshly smoked
  slivered chipotles or
  1 tablespoon pureed chipotle
  en adobo

Juice from 1 lime

1/3 cup tequila

1/2 teaspoon kosher salt

2 tablespoons minced cilantro

Lee James' Barbecued Chiles

On their northern California ranch, Lee James and her brother Wayne grow about 20 varieties of chiles. Wayne has trekked into the high mountains of Oaxaca to collect chile seeds. Their farm and chipotle smokehouse are so demanding, that summer entertaining has to be simple.

When the barbecue fire is medium hot, place cleaned chiles on the hot grill. Do not remove stems or slit chiles. It will take chiles almost 15 minutes to soften and char a little. Place a heavy griddle on one side of the grill.

Place several tortillas on the griddle with a stick of cheese in the middle of each. Place a couple of chipotle snippets on the cheese or a dab of adobo. When tortillas are warm and soft and cheese is melted, place on plates. Put a barbecued chile down the middle. If someone doesn't want the toasted skin on their chile, they can peel it off. To eat, just wrap the warm tortilla around the chile and bite down.

Stand around the barbecue with your chile and beer. Be happy.

LEE JAMES' BARBECUED CHILES

Assortment of fresh chiles:
Anaheim, New Mexican,
poblano
12 to 24 corn tortillas
depending on your crowd
1 to 2 pounds Monterey Jack
cut into sticks
2 to 4 freshly smoked chipotles
or pureed chipotle en adobo

Jerry's Halibut
2 large servings

I really should erect a shrine to Jerry George for being so insistent in his search for chipotles in Marin County that he helped talk Lee and Wayne James of Tierra Farms into smoking chiles in Grandma's castoff refrigerator. History was made and Jerry makes this halibut for everyone who will listen to his stories.

It's become a favorite of ours because: it has chipotles, it's easy, and has zero fat.

Jerry insists that the halibut be frozen since as it thaws in the oven, it slowly poaches in its own juices and the lime.

IMPORTANT!
Do not thaw halibut
before cooking.

Creations with Chipotles 35

JERRY'S HALIBUT

2 frozen halibut steaks (about
  1-1/4 pounds)

Zest from 1 lime

Juice from 3 limes

2 freshly smoked chipotles

1/2 teaspoon salt

1/2 cup minced cilantro

Place frozen halibut in a glass dish (13 x 9). Cover with zest, lime juice, and slivers of chipotle. It works best to cut chile slivers with scissors.

Use mild chipotles like the tam jalapeño if possible. If you are using moritas, they should first be soaked in hot water for 20 minutes before cutting into slivers. Discard seeds.

Sprinkle halibut with salt and cilantro. Bake in a preheated 350° oven for approximately 45 minutes. Check fish after thirty minutes. When perfectly done, it should barely flake when pierced with a fork. If your halibut steaks are thick, they could require a few more minutes.

Fire-With-Flavor Seasoning
3/4 cup (enough for 2 chickens)

Whenever I cook chicken to be included in other dishes like tacos, enchiladas, or torta filling I like it to have a lot of flavor. I devised Fire-With-Flavor to rub on the chicken before cooking and then finish with a simmer in beer. It's continued to be a favorite.

Place all ingredients into the bowl of a food processor. Grind together. Keeps well, stored in a glass jar if you have leftovers.

FIRE-WITH-FLAVOR SEASONING

2 teaspoons kosher salt

1 tablespoon cumin
powder

1 tablespoon minced
garlic

1 tablespoon onion powder

1 tablespoon dried oregano

1 tablespoon dried thyme

1 tablespoon dried epazote or
fresh if available

1 tablespoon New Mexican
ground red chile

2 chipotle or morita chiles or
smoke-dried New Mexican
chiles

Burnished Chicken
Serves 4 to 6

Eat Burnished Chicken over noodles, use for fajitas or tacos.

Cut the chicken into small pieces using sharp knife or poultry shears. Rub seasoning over all the surfaces. Place in glass bowl, cover with plastic wrap, and marinate for 1 to several hours.

Using a nonstick pan, barely coated with 1 or 2 teaspoons oil, sauté chicken in batches (3 batches is what I do) so it is lightly browned. Remove each batch to a plate as you continue sautéing. (If you load all the chicken in the pan at once, it will not brown very well.) Add more oil as needed for sautéing.

Put all the chicken back into the pan and add beer. Quickly put on the lid and allow chicken to steam about 5 minutes. Remove lid and continue cooking over medium high heat until beer cooks to a glaze that will coat the chicken. This chicken makes a great filling to include in enchiladas, burritos, over rice or in tortas. See below for suggested ideas.

BURNISHED CHICKEN

6 chicken breast filets, skinned

1/4 cup Fire-With-Flavor seasoning (recipe above)

1 tablespoon canola or olive oil, divided

1/2 cup beer

Burnished Chicken Tortas
or Sandwiches
Serves 2

Whenever I am preparing Burnished Chicken, I fix extra so that I can have leftovers for tortas and burritos. It keeps several days in the refrigerator or freezer, preserved nicely by all that chile and beer.

Spread mayonnaise on each bolillo half. Layer about 1/2 cup chicken on each bottom half of bolillos.

Cover chicken with onion slices, separated into rings, and next a layer of chopped lettuce. Finish off with slices of avocado and pickled jalapeño. Top with the other half of bolillo.

BURNISHED CHICKEN TORTAS OR

SANDWICHES

2 bolillos or Mexican Turtle Rolls, split

2 tablespoons mayonnaise (regular or reduced-fat)

1 heaping cup of leftover Burnished Chicken

2 slices mild onion, soaked briefly in ice water and blotted

1 cup chopped romaine or iceberg lettuce

1/2 avocado, sliced

2 to 4 pickled jalapeño chiles, sliced as for nachos (optional)

Veracruz Pork Tenderloins
Serves 4

In Veracruz, Mexico they rub pork shoulder with chile puree and wrap it in banana leaves before roasting; I have found a less traditional but equally as delicious way of cooking the little tenderloins by first rubbing them with Fire-With-Flavor spices. (See recipe page 37)

It's a good idea to double the recipe so you have extra spicy pork for burritos or soft tacos.

Preheat oven to 375° degrees. Squeeze lime juice over meat, drizzle with olive oil, and rub in Fire-With-Flavor spices.

Place tenderloins in an oiled, deep baking pan. Pour 1/2 cup beer in bottom of pan. Roast tenderloins for 45 minutes. Check every 15 minutes, moving the meat in the caramelized juices around the edges of the pan. Add the rest of the beer the last 15 minutes of cooking time and brush the tenderloins with the spicy beer in the pan.

If you want the tenderloins to be more browned, place them under a broiler for 5 minutes. Keep turning.

VERACRUZ PORK TENDERLOINS

2 pork tenderloins, about
  3/4 pound each
Juice of 1 lime
4 teaspoons olive oil
2 to 3 tablespoons
  Fire-With-Flavor Spice (see
  recipe page 37)
3/4 cup beer

Slice the tenderloins and serve with warm tortillas, black beans, and salsa. Also makes great sandwiches or tortas.

Mexican Turtle Rolls
10 Rolls

The key to good tortas is not just filling and garnishes, you have to have good bolillos or good teleras, the softer rolls that my family has nicknamed "Turtle Rolls" because they are shaped like a turtle shell. Since turtle rolls are wider than bolillos, you can cram in more filling.

You can buy these in a Mexican bakery or grocery store, but these darkly browned rolls taste even better when they come from your own oven.

1 tablespoon dry instant yeast

1/2 cup water

1 teaspoon sugar

1 cup evaporated milk

1 cup water

2 tablespoons brown sugar

2 tablespoons butter

2 teaspoons salt

2 cups bread flour

2-1/2 cups all purpose flour

*1/2 to 3/4 cup flour for
   kneading*

1 tablespoon melted butter

Dissolve the yeast in 108° warm water with sugar in a large mixing bowl. Let it proof until puffy.

Warm combined milk and remaining water to 110° and stir in brown sugar, butter, and salt. Add this mixture to the yeast. Then whisk in 2 cups bread flour until well blended. Slowly add the rest of the flour, 1/2 cup at a time. Knead dough on floured work surface for about 5 minutes. Put it back in bowl, cover with plastic wrap and let rise until doubled. This will take about an hour.

Punch the risen dough down and form into 10 balls. Roll each ball into an oblong shape. Place on greased baking sheet and flatten with your hand. To make the traditional telera marks, score the roll twice with long spatula, pressing all the way through the dough. This is what makes it look like the turtle shell (see photograph). Brush rolls with the melted butter and then if scoring disappears a little as the rolls rise, just mark them again with the spatula.

Let the rolls rise until almost doubled, about 35 minutes. Bake in a preheated 400° oven for 10 minutes and then turn oven to

375° and bake for another 15 minutes. Rolls will be a dark golden brown. Remove from baking sheets and cool for 1 hour. Place in plastic bags so crust will soften. Serve rolls the day of baking or freeze for up to 2 months.

Fiery Chimichangas
For 2 eaters

My first taster encountering these said, "These aren't chimichangas. They aren't greasy enough." These golden creations filled with spicy black beans and Burnished Chicken are like crisp turnovers. They are one more reason to keep batches of this spicy chicken stockpiled in your freezer.

Warm the flour tortillas in a hot ungreased skillet until they are soft and pliable. If you omit this step, the tortillas may crack when folded.

Place 1/2 cup beans in a little rectangle down the middle of each warmed tortilla. Sprinkle with 2 tablespoons grated cheese. Cover with 1/2 cup warmed chicken. Fold down top end toward the filling. Next fold over one side toward filling. Fold up bottom end and then fold over last side. Place on plate with all folds downward. This step can be done several hours in advance if needed. Cover folded chimichangas with plastic wrap.

FIERY CHIMICHANGAS

2 12-inch flour tortillas

1 cup leftover Black Bean Chili, warmed (recipe page 46)

1/4 cup grated Monterey Jack cheese (more if you like)

1 cup leftover Burnished Chicken (recipe page 38)

2 tablespoons canola oil

Heat a large skillet with the 2 tablespoons oil. When hot, carefully place both chimichangas, seams down, in skillet. Fry until golden brown, turning once. Immediately place on paper towels to drain. Blot off tops with more paper towels. Eat immediately as a snack or picnic.

You can fold the chimichangas several hours in advance, saving the frying until the last minute.
Be inspired as you add to the filling.
Just don't add ingredients that exude excessive juice that will leak out.
Also, don't do what I usually do and put in too much filling, making it difficult to fold the chimichanga properly.

Vegetarian Black Bean Chili
Serves 6

VEGETARIAN BLACK BEAN CHILI

1 pound black beans, rinsed
well, picked over for stones

9 cups water

1 sprig of epazote
(optional but good)

1 cup diced onion for
simmering with beans

3 bay leaves

1 chipotle, left whole

1 tablespoon olive oil

1-1/2 cups diced onion for
sautéing

1 jalapeño chile, seeded and
minced

1 tablespoon minced garlic

1 tablespoon oregano

3 teaspoons cumin seed

2 cups finely diced
tomatoes

As far as I am concerned there are never too many chili recipes and this one differs in that it requires a goodly amount of chipotle which adds a smokiness that subs for meat. I like to simmer black bean chili with one or two whole chipotles because of the "authority" a puffed up chile adds to the pot.

After rinsing black beans, place in pot with the water, epazote, onion, bay leaves, and whole chipotle. Bring to a boil and simmer for about 2 hours with lid partially on pot. Make sure that there is always enough water to cover beans sufficiently. If not, add hot water.

When beans are barely tender, drain off some of water and reserve. Next heat olive oil in skillet and fry onion and jalapeño until softened and then add garlic, oregano, cumin, and diced tomatoes.

Cook together 10 minutes and then add to the beans along with chile powder, chipotle puree, salt, and rice vinegar.

Simmer chili for another 30 to 45 minutes partially covered. Add some of reserved bean liquid back into pot if needed.

Serve Black Bean Vegetarian Chili in wide bowls, offering the garnishes so everyone can decorate their own chili.

*2 tablespoons excellent ground
   red chile*

2 tablespoons chipotle puree

1 to 2 teaspoons salt

1 tablespoon rice vinegar

Garnishes:

*1/2 cup minced green onions
   or mild red onions*

1/2 cup minced cilantro

*1/2 cup regular or reduced-fat
   sour cream*

Cooking the daily beans at Chileto's taqueria in Santa Barbara.

Sweet Fiery Baked Beans
Serves 6

Unless you come from Boston and are struck with some perverse loyalty, you may never want baked beans "that way" again. These are black, fiery with chipotle, and sweet. They go perfectly with anything barbecued or grilled. Since traditional baked beans are done with salt pork or bacon, these are great for fat-conscious eaters and vegetarians as the chipotle chiles give the smokiness usually provided by pork, but even better.

This is an adaptation of a recipe by Neil Stuart of Cafe Pacifica in San Diego

Simmer 1 pound of black beans (you don't have to soak them) with water, onion, bay leaves and epazot. Cooking time is about 1-1/2 hours or until beans are just barely tender.

Stir in the tomato puree, brown sugar, pureed chipotles, and vinegar. Bake in an oiled Dutch oven for about an hour at 375°. You want all the flavors to go into the beans.

SWEET FIERY BAKED BEANS

1 pound black beans, rinsed
well, picked over for stones
9 cups water
1 cup diced onion for
simmering with beans
3 bay leaves
1 sprig of epazote
1-1/2 cups tomato puree (like
Pomi)
1 cup brown sugar
2 tablespoons pureed chipotles
en adobo plus 1 teaspoon
salt
1/4 cup vinegar

A small street corner market in Oaxaca.

Turkey Chili
Makes 8 medium bowls of chili

This is a good chili to make when you want to be good (lower in fat that is) but not so good as to be vegetarian. The vegetables are "sautéed" in beer instead of the usual oil which is what makes this recipe special.

Simmer the beer, onion, bell pepper, garlic, bay leaves, oregano, and cumin in a 8-quart pot until beer is reduced by half.

Add the ground turkey to the beer mixture and simmer another 10 minutes. Break up the turkey during simmering; sprinkle with salt and pepper. Next add jalapeño slices.

TURKEY CHILI

12 ounces beer (do not use dark beer)

2 cups chopped onion

3/4 cup chopped red bell pepper

1-1/2 tablespoons minced garlic (yes, this is correct)

3 bay leaves

1 tablespoon dried oregano

1 tablespoon crushed cumin seeds

1 pound ground turkey

1/2 teaspoon salt

1/4 teaspoon freshly ground pepper

2 to 4 jalapeño chiles, seeded and sliced

Roughly puree tomatoes with their juices in a food processor. Add to the turkey-beer mixture. Stir in the chile powder and chipotle. Bring to a gentle simmer.

Cut the turkey tenderloins into 1/2-inch thick slices and cut into large dices. Add this diced turkey to the brewing pot. Simmer for thirty minutes. The raw turkey will release juices into the chili as it simmers adding flavor to the broth. Stir in the cooked beans and cook for another ten more minutes.

Blend masa harina into the 1/2 cup water to make a paste. Blend half of paste into the chili. If chili still needs more thickening, add the rest of the paste. Simmer for few more minutes and then stir in the cilantro.

Serve bowls of condiments such as sliced avocado or Avocado Salsa, olives, chopped red onions, more minced cilantro, and grated Cheddar cheese.

This chili is 340 calories a bowl and contains 6 grams of fat per serving, but this does not count condiments.

2 cans (18-3/4 ounces each) natural whole tomatoes with juice

1/4 cup New Mexican chile powder

2 teaspoons chipotle chile puree

2 turkey tenderloins

2 cups cooked black beans or substitute 2 cans (15 ounces each) black beans, drained

2 tablespoons masa harina for thickening

1/2 cup water

1/4 cup cilantro

Condiments:

Sliced avocados or Avocado Salsa (recipe follows)

Olives

Chopped red onions

Minced cilantro

Grated Cheddar cheese

Avocado Salsa
Makes about 2-1/2 cups salsa

Avocados are so frequently mashed into guacamole, it's a fresh approach to simply dice them instead and combine with other ingredients. Use perfectly ripened avocados as they won't dice very well if they are mushy.

Prepare about 30 minutes before serving time. First blister the jalapeño chiles over a flame. Place in brown bag or plastic bag so steam will loosen skins. After 5 minutes, peel off blackened skins. Cut chiles in half and use small knife to remove veins and seeds. Mince chiles.

Combine avocado with lemon juice, olive oil, green onion, jalapeños, garlic, salt, and cilantro. Cover salsa with plastic wrap which you remove just before serving. Serve as a garnish over chili, broiled chicken breasts, or fish. Or spoon over the tops of burritos.

AVOCADO SALSA

2 jalapeño chiles, seeded and minced

2 avocados, peeled and diced into cubes

2 tablespoons lemon juice

1 tablespoon virgin olive oil

2 green onions, minced

2 garlic cloves, minced

1/2 teaspoon salt

4 tablespoons cilantro, minced

Marlena's Garlic Bread
Serves 8

Marlena Spieler, the author of the *Hot and Spicy Cookbook*, knows her way around chile and is the inspiration here as I have adapted her Mexican-style garlic bread to include chipotle. I serve this bread with something simple like barbecued chicken or steaks and a salad; or simply pour a glass of wine and have the garlic bread for dinner!

Place the butter, olive oil, garlic, red chile, chipotle, and cilantro into the bowl of a food processor. Roughly puree. Spread half of the chile butter on each length of bread. If you like, use less garlic butter and reserve the rest for more bread later.

Arrange bread on baking sheet. You can make up the garlic bread several hours in advance if necessary and cover it with plastic wrap. Just before serving time, place baking sheet 8 inches under medium broiler. Heat until edges of bread are golden, about 4 to 5 minutes.

MARLENA'S GARLIC BREAD

1 stick butter, softened

2 tablespoons flavorful olive oil

4 cloves garlic, cut into pieces

1 tablespoon ground red chile

1 chipotle en adobo, 2 teaspoons chipotle puree, or 1 tablespoon slivered freshly smoked chipotle

2 tablespoons minced cilantro

1 loaf French bread, split lengthwise

The Authentic Cafe's Chipotle Eggs and Pan de Maíz
Serves 6

Ten years ago I first fell in love with chipotles. I used them mainly in salsas but carried on a search for more recipes. The most original and creative recipes were not coming from published cookbooks but from working chefs like Roger Hayot of the Authentic Cafe in Los Angeles. Eating out in small restaurants gave me more ideas.

It was fitting that I first encountered Roger, buying dried chiles in the Grand Central Market in Los Angeles. On our first visit to the Authentic Cafe for breakfast, we ordered the poached eggs over pan de maíz, smothered in Chipotle Gravy. It remains one of our favorite Mexican breakfast dishes. It is the kind of breakfast, we dream about if it's been too long since we've had it.

I shall always give Roger Hayot credit for being a chipotle pioneer.

Before you prepare anything else, soak the dried chiles for the Chipotle Gravy (see directions in the Chipotle Gravy recipe page 57). Then make the corn bread, so that it can be baking while you stir up the Chipotle Gravy.

When the corn bread is done, poach or lightly fry 1 or 2 eggs per person. Cut each person a large square of corn bread. Put eggs on top and cover with Chipotle Gravy (about 1/3 cup per serving).

Accompany with black beans, sausage and a side of chopped fruit to cool down the palate.

CHIPOTLE GRAVY OVER PAN DE
MAÍZ AND EGGS
6 squares of Pan de Maíz (see
  recipe below)
6 poached eggs
2-1/2 cups Chipotle Gravy (see
  recipe page 57)

Pan de Maíz or Corn Bread

This recipe makes enough corn bread and sauce for 6 people but you can fix just enough for 2 and have leftovers. It is a sweet, cake-like corn bread that goes well with the very picante sauce.

PAN DE MAÍZ OR CORN BREAD

1/4 cup melted butter

1/4 cup canola oil

1 cup whole or low-fat milk, slightly warmed

1 egg, room temperature

1 cup cake flour

1 tablespoon baking powder (preferably non-aluminum type)

2/3 cup yellow cornmeal

3 tablespoons sugar

1/2 teaspoon salt

Preheat oven to 400°. Oil a 9 x 13-inch baking dish or pan.

Combine melted butter, oil, milk, and egg in mixing bowl and whisk until well-blended.

Stir flour, baking powder, cornmeal, sugar, and salt together with a fork until blended. Add liquid ingredients to dry ingredients. Stir just until combined.

Pour into baking dish. Bake corn bread until golden on top and a tester inserted in middle comes out clean. Baking time is about 25 minutes.

Hint for hurried cooks: to an 8-1/2 ounce size Jiffy corn bread mix, add 1/2 cup evaporated milk or cream, 1 egg, and 1 tablespoon melted butter. Ignore what's called for on the package. Bake in greased pan for about 20 minutes in a preheated 400° oven.

Chipotle Gravy
Makes 2-1/2 cups

Roger Hayot prefers mora chiles. Moras are not as intensely smoky and seem to arrive in the United States a little fresher.

Rinse the chiles off to remove grit. Pour boiling water over 2 moras or chipotles and allow them to soak for at least 1 hour. When they have softened, puree them in a food processor with a small amount of water or chicken broth. You can use from 2 to 4 tablespoons.

Meanwhile, sauté shallots in olive oil and butter until softened. Then add flour and cook until lightly browned. Stir in the herbs and slowly whisk in milk and broth. Gently simmer for 5 minutes and then add the cream.

Simmer sauce for fifteen minutes or until slightly reduced and thickened. Next add 2 teaspoons chipotle puree and salt. Simmer 5 more minutes to concentrate flavors. If you want more chipotle flavor, add more puree at this point. It's picante.

CHIPOTLE GRAVY

1 to 2 reconstituted chipotle or mora chiles

2 tablespoons minced shallots

1 tablespoon olive oil

1 tablespoon butter

2 tablespoons flour

1/2 teaspoon dried sage

1 teaspoon dried thyme

1 cup milk

2/3 cup chicken broth

1/4 cup cream

1 to 2 reconstituted chipotle or mora chiles, pureed

1 teaspoon salt

Note:
Reserve leftover chipotle puree in a glass jar in refrigerator. You can blend it with mayonnaise and lime juice and use it as a sandwich spread.

Creations with Chipotles   57

Albóndigas en Salsa de Chipotle
Serves 6

One of the classic ways that chipotles are used in Mexico is with the meatballs known as albóndigas. There seems never to be enough sauce for dunking.

To prepare the Salsa de Chipotle, heat the olive oil in a large skillet and sauté the onion until translucent, about 5 minutes. Then add the garlic, tomatoes, broth, and chipotle puree. Simmer 20 minutes, then set aside while you complete the albóndigas.

ALBÓNDIGAS EN SALSA DE

CHIPOTLE

Salsa de Chipotle:

1 tablespoon olive oil

1 cup chopped onion

2 cloves minced garlic

1 (28-ounce) can crushed
  tomatoes with added puree

1-1/2 cups light chicken broth

2 tablespoons pureed chipotle
  en adobo

To prepare albóndigas, first soak bread in the milk for a minute and then squeeze out the milk and discard. Crumble the bread into a bowl containing both the ground sirloin and ground pork. Add the green onion, onion, parsley, egg, salt, oregano, pepper, nutmeg, and cinnamon. Use either a large spoon or your hands to blend all the ingredients together.

Form albóndigas about the size of golf balls. Preheat oven to 400°. Coat a roasting pan with olive oil spray and arrange albóndigas in pan. Bake for 20 minutes or until meatballs are lightly browned. Add them to the skillet containing the Salsa de Chipotle. Simmer for fifteen minutes. Serve immediately with rice, noodles, or fill Italian rolls for sandwiches.

When I am going to bring them to a tailgate picnic, I reheat the albóndigas in a chafing dish.

Albóndigas:

1 slice bread, crust removed

1/2 cup whole or low-fat milk

1 pound ground sirloin

1 pound ground pork (can substitute ground turkey for lower fat)

4 minced green onions

1/4 cup minced white onion

1/4 cup minced parsley

1 egg

1 teaspoon salt

1 teaspoon dried oregano

1/2 teaspoon pepper

1/4 teaspoon nutmeg

1/4 teaspoon cinnamon

Green Chile and Corn Chowder
8 servings

This thick, velvety chowder is perfect for a winter dinner.

1/2 pound chorizo Mexican
sausage or longaniza

2 tablespoons butter

1 cup chopped onion

1 cup diced red bell pepper

2 cups chicken stock

1 cup milk

3 cups diced red-skinned
potatoes

1/4 cup dried potato flakes

3 cups corn kernels

2 cups milk

1 teaspoon salt

2 Anaheim or New Mexican
green chiles, charred, skin
removed, and diced

1 whole chipotle chile

Fry chorizo in soup pot until fat is rendered. Drain chorizo on paper towels and reserve. Drain any grease from pot and wipe out. Heat butter in same pot and sauté onions and bell pepper until softened, about 5 minutes. Add chicken stock and milk to pot along with diced potatoes.

Simmer for 20 minutes or until potatoes are tender. Sprinkle the potato flakes on top of mixture; simmer for 5 minutes longer.

Next puree 1-1/2 cups of the corn kernels and 2 cups milk in blender. Add to the soup along with the remaining 1-1/2 cups whole corn kernels, salt, green chiles, and whole chipotle. Simmer on lowest heat for 15 minutes so that milk doesn't boil. During the last few minutes, add the reserved chorizo.

Optional step: blend chipotle puree into the sour cream and milk for garnish. Ladle the soup into wide bowls and drizzle a zig-zag Indian sign message of chipotle cream across the top of each serving of chowder.

Garnish (optional):
2 teaspoons pureed chipotle en adobo
1/4 cup sour cream plus 1 tablespoon milk

Caldo de Tlapeño
6 servings

While in a little Mexican restaurant eating a steaming bowl of the most delicious soup I had ever eaten, I was aware of something at once smoky and spicy. When I found out that the chipotle chile was the mystery ingredient, I was hooked. I first began my search for chipotles just so I could make Caldo de Tlapeño.

CALDO DE TLAPEÑO

1-1/2 quarts chicken broth

1 tablespoon minced garlic

*1 cup tomato puree or pureed
   roasted tomato*

2 teaspoons oregano

2 whole chipotles

*1 teaspoon ground red chile
   (New Mexican)*

*2 chopped stalks celery with
   leaves*

*1 pound boneless chicken
   breasts, broiled or grilled*

Salt and pepper

Combine chicken broth, garlic, tomato puree, oregano, chipotles, red chile, and celery in a large 4-quart pot. Simmer for 45 minutes to blend flavors. Just as the cooks do in Mexico, leave the chipotles whole. They will puff up and flavor the soup.

Meanwhile, salt and pepper the chicken breasts and broil or grill for 6 minutes on each side. When done, cut into strips and set aside.

Add the halved potatoes to the simmering broth and cook until tender, about 20 more minutes. Add the chicken strips. The soup can be prepared up to this point and held for 30 minutes or refrigerated.

A few minutes before serving time, bring the soup to a simmer and stir in the spinach, green onions, cilantro, and avocado cubes. Immediately, remove soup from the heat and ladle into wide bowls. This soup is an entire meal!

1 pound halved red-skinned
  potatoes
2 cups chopped fresh spinach
1/2 cup minced green onions
1/4 cup minced cilantro
1 sliced ripe avocado, cubed

Hint:
To roast tomatoes for soups and salsas place in oiled pan and bake at 400° for 20 minutes. Puree with pan juices in blender.

Chipotle Pizza With Red Onion, Cilantro, and Jack Cheese
Makes 2 12-inch pizzas

CHIPOTLE PIZZA WITH RED
ONION, CILANTRO, AND JACK
CHEESE

3/4 tablespoon active dry yeast
* or 1 packet dry active yeast*
1/3 cup warm water
1 teaspoon sugar
1-1/4 cup warm water
2 teaspoons honey
2-1/2 teaspoons salt
1 tablespoon olive oil
1/4 cup finely ground semolina
* or fine cornmeal*
3-1/2 cups unbleached all-
* purpose flour*

Stir yeast into 1/3 cup warm water (108°–110°) with sugar and proof for 5 minutes or until puffy.

In a large mixing bowl stir together the yeast mixture, the rest of warm water, honey, salt, olive oil, 1 cup flour, and semolina. Beat together with whisk. Then add the rest of the flour, a little at a time.

Put a little flour on a board and knead the pizza dough for 3 minutes.

Wash bread bowl, rub with olive oil, and return pizza dough to the bowl. Cover bowl with plastic wrap. Dough should double in about an hour.

While dough is rising, prepare the topping: sauté the onion in the olive oil until softened, about 5 minutes. Cut the chipotle into slivers and stir into the onion along with the cilantro and oregano. Preheat oven to 450°, 45 minutes in advance of baking.

Oil 2 heavy, dark baking sheets or pizza pans. Divide risen dough in half and punch down. Allow dough to rest 5 minutes to relax and then roll each half into a circle or free form shapes about 1/2-inch thick. Spread each pizza with the onion topping. Sprinkle with cheese. Bake pizzas for about 20 minutes or until golden brown around the edges.

Be experimental with these pizzas. When I have leftover Smoked Tomato Chipotle Salsa, I sometimes spread it over the top of the sautéed onions layered on the pizza. I sprinkle just 3 tablespoons of grated Parmesan or dry Monterey Jack over the top to make a Mexican pissaladiere. You can add more cheese, less cheese, or slivers of vegetables like sliced red bell pepper and jalapeño.

Topping:

4 cups sliced red onion

1 tablespoon olive oil

1 freshly smoked chipotle or chipotle reconstituted in hot water

2 tablespoons minced cilantro

1 tablespoon fresh oregano (preferably mild Greek oregano)

1 cup grated Monterey Jack cheese

Spicy Breadsticks
Makes 8 fat breadsticks

I love it when I can apply one recipe to make several different things. When I accidentally rolled out some pizza dough in an excessive amount of semolina (fine cornmeal). I noticed that after baking in a hot oven, the edges had the consistency of a crunchy breadstick.

By adding bits of chipotle, dried tomato and red peppers to the pizza dough, I made breadsticks with a boost of flavor. You can make them soft or crunchy depending upon the baking time.

Prepare the pizza dough up to the point where you have combined the yeast, water, sugar, the remaining 1-1/4 cups warm water, honey, salt, olive oil, and 1 cup flour. Using scissors, snip the chipotle chiles, dried tomato and peppers into small pieces. Stir this into the wet dough along with the garlic salt and then add the rest of the flour (about 3 cups) and 1/4 cup semolina.

SPICY BREADSTICKS

1 recipe of pizza dough (see previous recipe)

2 dried chipotle chiles, soaked in hot water until softened

2 tablespoons dried tomato, snipped into tiny pieces

3 tablespoons dried red or green bell pepper, snipped

1/2 teaspoon garlic salt

1/2 cup semolina or fine cornmeal, for sprinkling on work surface

Knead dough on floured surface for 5 minutes. Place dough back in bowl and cover tightly with plastic wrap. Let it rise until doubled, about 1 hour.

Punch dough down on floured work surface and pat into a 8 x 10 inch rectangle. Cut rectangle into 10 lengthwise pieces. Fold over each piece to smooth, and roll in the semolina to form breadsticks, 10 inches long. Be careful not to roll out longer than your baking sheets! Keep the work surface well-sprinkled with semolina.

Place breadsticks on well-oiled baking sheets. Let them rise 25 minutes. Bake in a preheated 425° oven for 10 minutes. Turn oven down to 400° and bake for another 15 minutes or until golden brown.

Serve with soups, salads, and stews. The breadsticks are also great dipped into thick salsa.

Salpicòn
Serves 4 as a dinner, 6 as an appetizer

According to my Spanish dictionary, salpicòn means splashing or throwing a little bit of everything together. Since Mexican cooks love to shred things, salpicòn can refer to beef, chicken, or seafood mixed with a lot of colorful ingredients. In this case, the dressing for the shredded beef salpicòn is a deep burnished adobe color and the prize ingredient is chipotle.

Park Kerr, an outrageous Texan who wrote the *Texas Border Cookbook* with his mother Norma Kerr, once told me that if I ever wanted to steal a recipe from him, I should steal his salpicòn. I didn't steal the whole recipe but just part of it. The part that included chipotle in the dressing. Thank you, Park.

I was not prepared to fall for salpicòn because the idea of a shredded beef salad did not even entice me and if I had not been working on it for my San Francisco Chronicle column, I probably wouldn't have tried it. By the time the shredded beef is combined with the Adobe Dressing, red onion, olives, tomatoes, cheese, and avocados it transcends just shredded beef.

Salpicòn can be eaten as a salad, it can be used as filling for soft tacos, or as a layer in a Mexican sandwich, the torta.

Enjoy!

Cut 3 slashes on each side of the flank steak, going against the grain. Rub in the garlic salt and pepper. Heat a heavy Dutch oven that has a lid. Add the olive oil. Brown the flank steak well on both sides. Browning adds flavor as opposed to just boiling the meat as is often done.

When the meat is browned, use a fork to rub the smashed garlic into the top. Add water and sliced onion to the pot and place on the lid. Simmer the meat for about 1 hour and 15 minutes. It should be quite tender.

Combine the ingredients for the Adobe Dressing: garlic, oregano, salt, pepper, olive oil, wine vinegar, lime juice, crushed tomatoes, chipotle puree, and diced fresh tomato.

Allow flank steak to cool for 15 minutes so you can handle it. Now this is where we differ from any traditional recipes which call for the meat to be shredded until it is threadlike. Slice the meat across the grain

SALPICÒN

1 flank steak, about 1-1/2 pounds

1 teaspoon garlic salt

1/2 teaspoon black pepper

2 teaspoons olive oil

2 cloves smashed garlic

2 cups water

1/4 cup sliced onion

Adobe Dressing:

(makes about 2 cups dressing)

2 cloves minced garlic

1 teaspoon dried oregano

1/2 teaspoon salt

1/4 teaspoon black pepper

1/4 cup flavorful olive oil

1/3 cup red wine vinegar

2 tablespoons lime juice

1/3 cup canned crushed tomatoes in puree

1/4 cup pureed chipotles en adobo

1/2 cup fresh tomato, seeded

and diced

into 2-inch strips. Using 2 forks, pull the meat apart until it is shredded but in big shreds. Mix the shredded meat with half of the Adobe Dressing. Reserve the rest of the dressing to pass at the table.

Now stir in the diced red onion, tomatoes, black olives, diced cheese, and cilantro. Drizzle 1/4 cup more dressing on top. Place the salpicòn in a large flat dish and stick the romaine leaves around the edges. Garnish more with sliced avocado and tomato. Serve with warm corn tortillas and beans. Pass the remaining dressing at the table to be added as desired.

Each person spoons a little salpicòn into a tortilla and swoons in happiness. Perfect supper for a summer night or an appetizer preceding a barbecue.

Remaining Salpicòn
  Ingredients:
1/2 cup diced red Bermuda
  onion
2 tomatoes, seeded and diced
1/2 cup black olives, sliced
1/2 cup diced Monterey Jack
  cheese or queso ranchero
1/2 cup minced cilantro
6 inner leaves of romaine
  lettuce
1 avocado, skinned, pitted, and
  sliced
1/4 cup cherry tomatoes, sliced
  in half
12 corn tortillas for 4 people
  (more tortillas for 6 people)

Hearts of Romaine with Adobe Dressing
Serves 4 to 6

Remove tough, outer leaves of romaine. Discard or reserve for another salad. Arrange rest of romaine leaves on a platter. Dip the cherry tomato halves in the minced cilantro. Place the palm hearts and cherry tomatoes on top of lettuce. Drizzle salad with two-thirds of the Adobe Dressing (see recipe page 69) and pass the rest at the table. Sprinkle the cotijo cheese over the top of the salad as a snowy garnish. This is a beautiful, refreshing salad that accompanies grilled fish, steak or chicken.

Cotijo cheese is a crumbly, tangy cheese that may also be called queso ranchero or queso fresco. It is similar to feta cheese which can be used as a substitute. In Mexico, cotijo or queso fresco is crumbled in small amounts over beans, enchiladas, or salads.

HEARTS OF ROMAINE WITH

ADOBE DRESSING

1 head of romaine lettuce, washed and blotted dry
1 cup cherry tomatoes, halved
1/4 cup finely minced cilantro
1/2 cup palm hearts, sliced (optional but good)
Adobe Dressing (see recipe page 69)
1/2 cup crumbled queso cotijo or feta cheese

Milly's Creamy Orange Chipotle Dressing
16 ounces dressing or enough for 4 salads

In San Rafael, California there is a wonderful vegetarian restaurant called Milly's where they have found a way to disguise tofu—with chipotles! This dressing is one of the best uses I have found for tofu.

In blender, puree to sauce consistency: the tofu, lime, and orange juices, salt, cilantro, honey, and chipotle. Refrigerate until ready to use. Keeps 5 days.

Serve over simple tossed salad or Southwestern Salad with Toasted Pepita (see following recipe).

MILLY'S CREAMY ORANGE

CHIPOTLE DRESSING

1 (10 ounce) box Mori-nu firm
  tofu or Mori-nu lite
1/2 cup freshly squeezed lime
  juice (about 4 limes)
1/3 cup fresh orange juice
1 teaspoon kosher salt
3/4 cup cilantro leaves
1-1/2 tablespoons honey
1 chipotle, reconstituted in hot
  water for 10 minutes

Southwestern Salad with Toasted Pepitas
Serves 4 to 6

Tear the romaine into bite size pieces. Cut orange into thin slices and arrange with jicama on top of lettuce. Drizzle with dressing and sprinkle with pepitas just before serving.

Pepitas are hulled pumpkin seeds usually sold raw and untoasted. They puff when toasted and develop wonderful flavor. To toast them, place 1 cup raw pepitas in a heavy, nonstick skillet. Spray them lightly with olive oil spray. Sprinkle 3 teaspoons sugar over bottom of pan. The sugar will liquefy and lightly coat the pepitas as you stir them around the pan. After pepitas are toasted and puffed (this takes from 5 to 8 minutes), turn off the heat, and sprinkle nuts with 1 teaspoon kosher salt and 1 teaspoon good red chile powder (like New Mexican or Dixon). Stir and cool before using.

1 head of romaine lettuce, washed and dried

1 peeled Navel orange, white pith removed

1 cup jicama cut into matchsticks

1/2 cup Creamy Orange Chipotle Dressing (see previous recipe)

1/3 cup toasted pepitas (see recipe note)

Creations with Chipotles   73

Spicy Caesar Salad
Serves 4

This salad is a great way to spike up something that is already one of our favorites.

SPICY CAESAR SALAD

2 teaspoons anchovy paste
  (found in tube)
2 teaspoons finely minced
  garlic
1 tablespoon Dijon mustard
3 tablespoons lemon juice
1 tablespoon pureed
  chipotle en adobo
1/3 cup fruity olive oil
1 head romaine lettuce, washed
  and dried will; torn to small
  pieces
1/4 cup grated Asiago cheese
1/2 cup croutons or slivered,
  toasted tortillas

Blend together the anchovy paste, garlic, mustard, lemon juice, chipotle, and olive oil; a food processor works well for blending or you can simply use a fork. Toss half of Caesar dressing with lettuce, adding more if needed. Sprinkle with grated cheese and croutons. Reserve rest of dressing for another salad or to be added as needed.

*Note on toasting tortillas:
Spray olive oil mist on both
sides of 2 corn tortillas. Cut
each into narrow strips. Toast
in 375° oven for about
8 minutes.*

Barbecued Chicken Tinga

There are certain Mexican folk dishes such as tinga that cry out for the powerful hit of the chipotle chile without which there would be no tinga. Tinga is kind of a combination stew-picadillo and is sufficiently warm enough to be felt all the way to the ear lobes. But don't let that scare you away as you can tone it down by decreasing the amount of chipotle although you won't catch me decreasing the heat!

Tinga can be served as a winter stew, a filling for burritos and empanadas, or in tortas (Mexican sandwich made in a bolillo or French roll). The flavors improve and intensify after a couple of days, making tinga the perfect make-ahead dish.

BARBECUED CHICKEN TINGA

2 tablespoons lime juice

1 tablespoon flavorful olive oil

1 teaspoon garlic salt

4 chicken thighs, skinned

4 chicken breasts, skinned

1 tablespoon oil for sautéing

2 cups chopped onion

4 cloves minced garlic

1/4 pound lean Mexican
   chorizo sausage

2 pounds tomatoes (about 4
   large tomatoes)

1/2 cup tomato puree (like
   Pomi) for thickening

2 tablespoons chipotle puree

1 bay leaf

1 teaspoon dried oregano

1 tablespoon brown sugar

1/2 teaspoon salt

Blend lime juice, olive oil, and garlic salt. Marinate chicken in this for at least an hour. Start the charcoal in your barbecue grill so the coals will be covered with white ash when you are ready for grilling chicken. Alternatively, use a gas barbecue grill.

In a large skillet, heat oil and sauté onions until softened. At the last minute add the garlic and sauté for only a couple of minutes longer. Remove the onions and garlic and add the chorizo to the pan. Sauté until browned. Blot as much fat as possible out of the pan using paper towels. Return the onions and garlic to the pan with the chorizo.

Place tomatoes on a baking sheet and broil just until skins are loosened or turn over a gas flame to slightly char surface. Set aside to cool.

Skin tomatoes. Halve them and squeeze out seeds. Chop tomatoes and add to the skillet along with the canned tomato puree, chipotle puree, bay leaf, oregano, and brown sugar. Simmer for 20 to 30 minutes. Add salt. This sauce can even be done the day before.

Grill the chicken: the chicken breasts should be given about 8 minutes per side and the thighs about 15 to 20 minutes per side. Remove cooked chicken from grill. Cut the breasts into strips and cut the meat off the thighs. Add chicken to the tinga sauce along with the diced potatoes. Simmer everything together for only 10 minutes.

Garnish with avocado. This is quite wonderful spooned into warm corn tortillas and eaten as soft tacos.

4 red-skinned new potatoes,
cooked until just tender and
diced into cubes

Garnish:
1 avocado, sliced

In a small Oaxacan market, chickens are sold with feet!

Tinga Poblana
Serves 6

In Mexico, Tinga Poblana is done using pork, especially the flavorful but high fat pork shoulder. I have substituted the leaner pork tenderloins and the stew is still delicious although a bit nontraditional.

Preheat oven to 350°. Prepare meat first so that it can be roasting while you do everything else. Dry tenderloins with paper towels. Rub with minced garlic, salt, pepper, and oregano. Heat oil in heavy Dutch oven and brown meat well. It should be brown on all sides as this step will add more flavor. In traditional tinga, the pork is usually boiled. After browning, add the bay leaves, onion, cloves, and water to the pot. Cover pot and place in oven for 1-1/2 hours. Check pot a couple of times to make sure there is sufficient liquid in the pot. Add another 1/2 cup water if necessary.

Remove cooked tenderloins from pot. Don't wash pot and reserve any remaining liquid for later cooking of tinga sauce. Cut meat into slices while still warm and pull meat apart into thick shreds.

TINGA POBLANA

2 pork tenderloins, about 1
   pound each
2 cloves garlic, minced through
   a press
1 teaspoon salt
1/2 teaspoon freshly ground
   black pepper
2 teaspoons dried oregano,
   crushed
1 tablespoon olive oil
2 bay leaves
1 onion halved and stuck with 4
   cloves
1-1/2 cups water

Tinga Sauce

Make the tinga sauce while the tenderloins are roasting.

Broil or char tomatoes to loosen skins. Remove skins and halve the tomatoes. Squeeze out seeds. Place tomatoes into the bowl of a food processor with garlic, cut into pieces, and the chipotle chiles. Chop to a coarse puree. If you are using canned tomatoes place along with their juices in the food processor with garlic and chipotles.

Heat the olive oil in large skillet and sauté onions for 5 minutes or until softened. Remove and set aside. Using same skillet, fry the chorizo for about 5 minutes. Blot with paper towels and blot up any excess fat in skillet. Return the onions to skillet with the chorizo. Add the tomato-chipotle mixture along with the vinegar, brown sugar, salt, adobo juice, bay leaves, and spices. Simmer for twenty minutes to concentrate flavors.

Add the tinga sauce to the shredded tenderloins and remaining broth. Simmer for twenty minutes. If mixture seems too dry, add 1/2 cup water or broth.

Tinga Sauce:

5 large, ripe tomatoes or 1 can plum tomatoes (28 ounces)

3 cloves garlic

2 chipotle chiles adobado (from can or jar)

2 teaspoons olive oil

2 medium onions, about 1-1/2 cups

1/2 pound lean, bulk Mexican chorizo sausage

2 tablespoons apple cider vinegar

2 tablespoons brown sugar

1/2 teaspoon salt

2 teaspoons adobo sauce from can or jar

2 bay leaves

1/2 stick cinnamon bark

1/4 teaspoon cloves

Garnishes:

2 avocados, sliced

1 red onion, sliced thinly and
   separated into rings

Shredded lettuce

Pickled jalapeños

Serve the Tinga Poblana garnished with avocado slices and red onion rings. You can alternatively serve tinga in hollowed out bolillos or Italian rolls. Add the sliced onion, avocado, shredded lettuce, and pickled jalapeños.

Tomatillo Morita Salsa
Makes about 4 cups salsa

This typically Mexican salsa of Ernesto Mendoza of La Sandia Azul in Mexicali combines the green husk tomatoes (tomatillos) and smoked chiles, an addictive combination. I will give you the recipe for the salsa first and then give you several delicious ways to use it.

Soak morita chiles in boiling water for 30 minutes. Meanwhile, prepare rest of ingredients. Fry the chopped onion in an ungreased frying pan (nonstick is preferable) until slightly browned but not burned. Add the garlic toward the end so it doesn't burn.

Place tomatillos in hot water to help soften husks. Remove husks. Cut tomatillos in half.

Place onions, garlic, tomato, tomatillos, soaked moritas, water, chipotle puree and rice vinegar in blender and puree.

Place puree in saucepan and simmer for 15 minutes. Taste for seasoning and add salt if needed.

Note:
Ernesto uses from 6 to 8 more morita chiles for a much hotter salsa.

TOMATILLO MORITA SALSA

2 morita chiles

1 cup chopped onions

3 cloves garlic

1 pound tomatillos

1 medium large tomato, broiled or charred over flame

1/2 cup water seasoned with 1 teaspoon Maggi chicken granules

1 to 2 teaspoons pureed chipotles en adobo

1 teaspoon rice vinegar

1/2 teaspoon salt

San Francisco Crab Enchiladas with Tomatillo Morita Salsa
6 enchiladas

SAN FRANCISCO CRAB

ENCHILADAS WITH TOMATILLO

MORITA SALSA

2 teaspoons canola oil

1 cup chopped sweet onion (red Bermuda or Vidalia)

1-1/2 cups flaked crab meat (Dunguness if possible)

1/2 pound grated Monterey Jack cheese

6 corn tortillas

1 to 2 tablespoons canola oil for frying tortillas

2 cups reserved Tomatillo Morita Salsa (see recipe page 81)

Garnishes:

Sour Cream Cilantro Sauce (recipe follows)

1/4 cup black olives

1 sliced avocado

There are two crucial factors in making enchiladas. First you must seal the tortillas with oil and heat. If you don't seal them, the enchiladas are likely to disintegrate as soon as the sauce penetrates the tortilla. A corn tortilla is made up of a water-based corn dough, making it very fragile when exposed to more water, salsa or enchilada sauce. Secondly, it is really important to just heat the rolled enchilada. If you bake enchiladas over 15 minutes they can start to disintegrate and become a casserole. In Mexico, enchiladas most often are rolled up, doused with warm sauce and toppings and served.

Heat the small amount of oil and sauté the onion until softened but not browned. Set aside with the rest of the filling: the crab meat and the grated cheese.

Prepare the tortillas by frying them in as small amount of oil as possible. Use 1 to 2 teaspoons oil per tortilla in a nonstick pan. Fry each tortilla about a minute, until it is softened and both sides are sealed. Stack the prepared tortillas on a plate. Complete this step right before rolling up the enchiladas.

Place the Tomatillo Morita Salsa in a shallow bowl. Dip each softened tortilla in the salsa and then place it on a flat plate. Place filling down the center: a heaping tablespoon of sautéed onion, 1/4 cup crab, a teaspoon of salsa, and a tablespoon of cheese. Fold over each side of enchilada. Place enchiladas seam down in an oiled baking dish. Do not crowd.

When all the enchiladas are completed, cover with any leftover salsa and the remaining grated cheese. Heat in a preheated 400° oven for 8 to 10 minutes.

Serve garnished with Sour Cream Cilantro Sauce, olives, and avocado slices.

Sour Cream Cilantro Salsa
1 cup salsa

Stir green onion, garlic, cilantro into sour cream. Season to taste with salt. Reserve in refrigerator until needed for enchilada topping. Is also good over burritos and even baked potatoes.

SOUR CREAM CILANTRO SALSA

1 minced green onion

1 minced garlic clove

2 tablespoons minced cilantro

1 cup sour cream, regular or
  reduced fat

Ernesto's Sauté of Filete in Tomatillo Morita Salsa
2 to 4 servings

The Tomatillo Morita Salsa is also delicious with this sauté of filete. It makes a wonderful quick meal that only needs to be rolled up into warm corn tortillas. Use a tender cut of beef because it should only be cooked briefly. For more servings, just increase amount of meat and amount of salsa.

Sauté onion in olive oil for a couple of minutes and then push to the side of pan and add garlic and meat. Fry until lightly browned, about 10 minutes. Add the salsa to the pan and cover. Simmer for another 10 minutes so that the juices may enhance the salsa. Taste for seasoning.

Meanwhile, warm the tortillas (and make a light salad). Dinner's ready.

Pinch of salt

ERNESTO'S SAUTÉ OF FILETE IN TOMATILLO MORITA SALSA

1/2 cup chopped onion

1 tablespoon olive oil

2 cloves minced garlic

1 pound filete or New York steak, cut into small pieces

1 cup Tomatillo Morita Salsa (see recipe page 81)

Pinch of salt and black pepper

Lots of corn tortillas

Ranch Enchiladas

Makes 12 enchiladas for 6 hungry people

The sauce for these northern Mexican style enchiladas is the kind that people keep wanting to dip into so if there is any left, I serve a bowl of it at the table.

First prepare the Chipotle Cream: heat the butter until bubbling and then stir in the flour. Cook the roux over very low heat for 2 minutes.

To the roux, add the cumin, oregano, garlic, chipotles, green chiles, and chicken broth. Simmer gently on low heat for at least twenty minutes.

Prepare your enchilada fillings. Mince onions and grate the cheese. Soften and seal your tortillas by frying them 1 at a time in a small amount of oil (1-2 teaspoons at a time) in nonstick pan. Set aside while you finish the sauce.

Remove the simmered sauce from heat and blend in the sour cream.

Lay softened tortilla on a flat plate, and place filling down the center: a heaping teaspoon of minced onion and a heaping tablespoon of cheese. Fold over sides and place

RANCH ENCHILADAS

Chipotle Cream:

2 tablespoons butter

2 tablespoons flour

1 teaspoon toasted cumin

1-1/2 teaspoons oregano

3 cloves minced garlic

*2 to 3 tablespoons pureed
   chipotles adobado*

*2 green chiles (Anaheim or
   New Mexican type): charred,
   skins removed, and chopped*

2 cups chicken broth

*1/2 cup sour cream, regular or
   reduced fat*

Filling:

1 cup minced onion

*12 ounces of grated
   Chihuahua, Kasseri, or
   Italian fontinella cheese*

12 corn tortillas

*2 to 3 tablespoons canola oil
   for frying corn tortillas*

enchilada, seam down, on oiled baking sheet. Cover each enchilada with Chipotle Cream. Sprinkle with remaining grated cheese. Place in hot 400° oven for just 5 minutes and serve.

Velvet Chipotle Salsa For Enchiladas
Makes about 3 cups

This is my version of a sauce served in Seranata de Garibaldi, a small family-run restaurant in East L.A. whose owner-chef, Sr. Jose Rodriguez, was recently called a *maestro de salsas* by *Gourmet* magazine.

This is one of the most exquisite sauces to make with chipotle; very French in character and very Mexican in soul.

I would not dare ask Sr. Rodriguez for one of his best secrets and so I worked hard to come up with a sauce as complex and rich as the Chipotle Salsa that envelops his seafood (or chicken enchiladas). In comparison to the Chipotle Cream recipe given above, this sauce is deeper, more complex, and therefore more time-consuming to make.

This is such a heavenly sauce and one which demonstrates that Mexican food can be complex and delicate at the same time. I make up the chipotle-tomato puree and keep it for a couple of weeks at a time in the refrigerator. When I need to make enchiladas, I then simmer the puree with the cream so the salsa has a fresh taste.

First pour boiling water over the dried chiles and soak for at least 30 minutes or more. You can also microwave the chiles in water to cover for 2 minutes on high power and let them soak. While chiles are soaking, prepare the rest of the ingredients.

Place half an onion and a head of garlic (yes, an entire head) with the top sliced off on a square of aluminum foil. Drizzle olive oil over onion and garlic. Wrap up the foil tightly. Bake for 45 minutes at 375°.

Cut tomatoes in half and place in 3-quart pot along with the water, sprig of thyme and the soaked chiles. Add the roasted onion and head of garlic. Simmer partially covered for 45 minutes.

VELVET CHIPOTLE SALSA FOR

ENCHILADAS

3 chipotle chiles or 5 morita chiles

1 guajillo chile (or dried California chile)

1/2 of large, flat red onion

1 head of garlic, top sliced off to expose cloves

2 teaspoons olive oil

2 medium tomatoes (about 1/2 pound)

3 cups water (or use half chicken broth, half water)

1 sprig fresh thyme

1/2 cup half and half cream

1/2 to 1 teaspoon salt

Puree the following ingredients in a food processor: the cooked tomatoes, chiles, half of the cooked onion, 3 cloves of the cooked garlic, and half of the simmering liquid from the pot.

Push the puree through a strainer placed over a large bowl so that the chile skins and tomato skins are removed. Place the puree back into the pot. Add the half and half cream and simmer the sauce for 3 to 5 minutes to reduce and thicken it a little. Stir in salt.

To make the salsa even more velvety for special occasions, stir in 2 tablespoons heavy cream just at the end of simmering. I think this is what the estimable Sr. Rodriquez does.

Use this salsa for the Stacked Vegetarian Enchiladas or Seafood Enchiladas (recipes follow).

Stacked Vegetarian Enchiladas
4 enchiladas

What I truly love about New Mexican-style stacked enchiladas is that they can be assembled right at your burners with no need for tucking, rolling, and baking. Utter simplicity and speed. In fact, these particular enchiladas were created the day I was on a test run for the salsa and we wanted to taste it with enchiladas which were put together in minutes—just like they do the street enchiladas over one brazier in the zocalos of Mexico.

The Velvet Chipotle Salsa should be simmering in a wide shallow pan. Keep the salsa on low heat and then turn it off when it is sufficiently hot.

The onion should be chopped and waiting and the cheese grated and waiting. You are going to move fast. You could even use 2 skillets to heat the tortillas if you want to be really fast.

Heat 1 teaspoon of oil at a time in a large nonstick skillet. Fry 2 tortillas at a time just so that they are softened and sealed. Give them less than a minute on each side.

STACKED VEGETARIAN

ENCHILADAS

1-1/2 cups Velvet Chipotle
Salsa (see recipe page 88)
2 cups roughly chopped mild
onion, like red Bermuda
2 cups grated Monterey Jack
2 tablespoons canola oil to be
used in small amounts
12 fresh corn tortillas

Garnish:
Halved cherry tomatoes
Avocado sliced
Cilantro

Have dinner plates waiting. Use tongs to dip each tortilla into the hot Velvet Chipotle Salsa and then lay the first tortilla onto a plate. Sprinkle with some chopped onion and cheese. Cover this with the next softened and dipped tortilla. Sprinkle with more grated cheese and onion. Lastly, lay on the next fried and dipped tortilla. Spoon more wonderful salsa over the top of the finished enchiladas. Garnish tops with a little grated cheese. Assemble all of the stacked enchiladas in this manner, serving them as they are assembled or keep warm in a 250° oven. Don't keep in a warming oven for any longer than 10 minutes.

Garnish with something red like halved cherry tomatoes and slices of avocado and cilantro.

Seafood Enchiladas With Velvet Chipotle Salsa
8 enchiladas

2 teaspoons olive oil

1 cup chopped mild onion

1 teaspoon Greek or
Mediterranean oregano

2 cups combination of
seafood: poached firm fish
like halibut, cooked lobster,
crab, shrimp, scallops, or
even just poached chicken

2 cups Velvet Chipotle Salsa
(see recipe page 88)

2 tablespoons canola oil

8 large corn tortillas

1 cup grated Monterey Jack
cheese or fontinella cheese
for filling

1 cup grated Monterey Jack
cheese for topping

Heat the olive oil in a nonstick skillet and sauté the onion until softened. Add the oregano. Stir in the seafood and remove skillet from heat. Heat the chipotle salsa so that it is bubbling and then remove from heat.

Using just 1 teaspoon of canola oil at a time in a nonstick skillet, fry each corn tortilla until softened and sealed. After all of the tortillas have been softened, place one at a time on a flat plate or work surface. Place 1/4 cup of the onion-seafood mixture down middle. Drizzle a couple of teaspoons salsa over the seafood and then sprinkle with a tablespoon of cheese. Fold over each side of the enchilada. Place enchilada seam side down in a greased baking pan. Do not place the enchiladas close together or they might stick to one another. Spoon salsa over each enchilada so is completely covered. Sprinkle the grated cheese over the tops. Bake in a hot 400° oven for no more than 10 minutes.

If I am lucky enough to have lobster or shrimp, I don't put it all inside the enchiladas for filling, I reserve some to place on tops of the enchiladas.

Green Corn Tamales
Makes about 16 tamales

GREEN CORN TAMALES

12 ears corn

Fresh corn husks

3/4 cup to 1 cup yellow
   cornmeal

1/2 cup softened butter

1/4 cup sugar(you can reduce
   sugar if your corn is sweet)

1-1/2 teaspoons salt

1/4 cup half and half or cream

Parchment cut into 8" x 12"
   rectangles

16 pieces of cotton string cut
   into 2 foot lengths

Filling:

8 ounces Cheddar cheese cut
   into 16 pieces

1 7-ounce can green chiles,
   drained and cut into strips

These are the tamales of summer and best made with fresh corn. El Cholo, a restaurant that has been an institution in Los Angeles since 1929, is famous for its green corn tamales which are only made from June to September. When I asked the chef why they couldn't use the corn from the Coachella Valley in winter, he looked at me like I was crazy and said, "Then they wouldn't be special cause you could have them any time. This way everyone looks forward to June." The tamales below are very close to El Cholo's version right down to the method for tying into a neat package with parchment.

The tamales are sweeter than traditional masa tamales and are sort of like little corn puddings filled with green chile and cheese.

First carefully remove green husks from corn by trimming off each end of cob. Unfurl the husks by peeling them off carefully. Only keep the larger husks and discard the inner, small husks. You will need about 3 husks for each tamale. Place husks in the sink. Pour boiling water over them and allow them to soak while you are working on other ingredients.

To cut off corn, stand ear of corn in a large bowl and cut off the kernels. Place half the kernels at a time into the bowl of a food processor and grind with half the cornmeal.

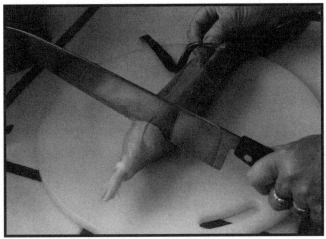

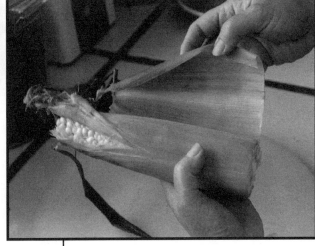

Place this puree into a large mixing bowl and then grind the rest of kernels and cornmeal together.

Add the butter, sugar, salt, and cream to the last batch and grind together. Stir this into the first puree until well-blended. If the mixture seems too liquid, add up to 1/4 cup more cornmeal to thicken.

Have all of your essential items laid out: the drained corn husks, the cut pieces of parchment, cotton string, and the filling ingredients. Overlap 3 husks. Scoop 1/4 cup corn mixture onto the middle of the husks and press a piece of cheese into the corn, cover with a couple strips of chile, and a tablespoon of corn mixture on top.

Fold over the sides of the husks. Lastly fold down the top of husks. The corn should be enclosed. You will have to use one hand to hold the husks into a packet which you now place into the middle of the parchment rectangle. Fold over bottom and top of the rectangle and then the sides.

Tip:
Corn juices may leak out.
Blot around edge of filling
with paper towel.

Tie the cotton string as you would a package. Place tamale on a tray while you fold and package the rest.

Instead of making individual tamales you can pour the corn mixture into a casserole dish. Press chiles, cheese, and several soaked cornhusks into top. Bake at 350° for 35 to 40 minutes.

Lay tamales on a steamer. I use a 2-layered Chinese steamer and place 8 tamales on each level. Steam for 50 minutes. Serve immediately or cool and then place in plastic and freeze. They keep well in freezer for 3 months which is a good plan when you have a lot of help to make several batches of tamales.

Eat Green Corn Tamales as they are or serve with a variety of salsas: fresh tomato salsa, mole, custard sauce, or the Chipotle Cream Salsa given below.

Chipotle Cream Salsa
Makes about 2/3 cup salsa

CHIPOTLE CREAM SALSA

2 tablespoons minced shallots

1/2 cup white wine

2 tablespoons cream

2 to 3 teaspoons pureed
chipotle en adobo or slivers
of freshly smoked chipotles or
smoked chile pasado

1/2 cup sour cream (you may
use reduced-fat sour cream)

Sauté the shallots in the wine until wine is reduced by half. Add the cream and chipotle and simmer a minute longer. Remove from heat and stir in the sour cream. Drizzle a few teaspoons over the top of the green corn tamales.

Smoked Chicken Chipotle Tamales
Makes 12 large tamales

This is one of my favorite tamale recipes because you have the rich chipotle flavors coming from every layer: the masa dough, the filling, and if you choose to make it, the Smoky Corn Salsa for topping (recipe page 103). I love the Nicaraguan nacatamales which contain surprises of olives, raisins, capers, rice, potatoes, and anything else that is the cook's whim and so I have "borrowed" from that filling.

Smoked Chicken Chipotle Tamales are an inspiration based on a recipe by Michele Anna Jordan, the author of *Oil and Vinegar* and *A Cook's Tour of Sonoma*. She is a very creative cook who seems to love chipotles also.

SMOKED CHICKEN CHIPOTLE

TAMALES

1 package of corn husk or
hojas

24 pieces of cotton string, cut
into 2-foot lengths

Tamale dough:

1/3 cup lard

2 cups masa harina (dehy-
drated masa)

1 teaspoon baking powder

1 teaspoon salt

1/2 cup canola oil

2 tablespoons pureed chipotles
en adobo

1-1/2 cups hot chicken broth

Since you will be needing several table-spoons chipotle puree, it will make it easier if you begin the recipe by pureeing a whole can of chipotles en adobo in your food processor. Reserve for this recipe and others.

Soak the corn husks in a sink filled with hot water to soften and clean them.

Prepare tamale dough by first beating the lard into the dry ingredients: the masa flour, baking powder, and salt. Slowly drizzle in the oil, the chipotle puree, and the hot broth. Beat the dough about 2 minutes or until it makes a slapping noise against the bowl of the mixer. If the dough does not make a slapping noise, it is not moist enough and you need to add a little more liquid.

Important!
Add one tablespoon of liquid at
a time.

The dough should not be runny. It should resemble thick biscuit dough.

Set the completed dough aside while you prepare the filling. Sauté onion in oil until softened, about 5 minutes on medium heat. Stir in the minced garlic, chicken, pureed chipotle, broth, capers, olives, and raisins. Simmer for 3 minutes to blend flavors. At the last minute, add the diced potatoes and cilantro. Salt the filling to your taste. This same filling is also good inside state-of-the-art tacos.

Tamale assembly: cut 24 pieces of cotton string in 2-foot lengths. Drain the wet husks on paper towels. If the husks aren't wide, overlap two husks. Spread about 1/4 cup masa dough on the middle of the husks and up to 1-inch from the sides. Leave the ends of the husks free so that you may tie the ends without dough squeezing out. Place 1/4 cup filling into center of dough. If you happen to have large husks, you'll be able to use more dough and more filling. Fold the sides of the tamale over and tie ends with a piece of string. My grandmother used to spread a layer of masa

Filling:

1 tablespoon canola oil or olive oil

1 cup diced onion

4 cloves minced garlic

1-1/2 cups coarsely chopped smoked chicken (leftover roasted chicken can be substituted)

2 tablespoons pureed chipotles en adobo

1/4 cup chicken broth

3 teaspoons capers

1/2 cup sliced black olives

1/3 cup raisins

1 cup diced, cooked potato

2 tablespoons minced cilantro

Salt to taste

dough on additional husks and wrap them around the center tamale. This makes a huge tamale to beat all tamales and is great for people who love the masa. You'd have to double the recipe for masa dough if you wanted to do this.

Your steaming pot or tamale pot should be waiting on the stove with the bottom layer filled with a couple of inches of boiling water. Lay the tamales on the rack of the steamer. It's okay if you lay some tamales on top of one another. Steam tamales for 50 minutes. If you made small tamales, they will be done in less time. Check after 40 minutes.

Serve tamales immediately or after cooling, wrap in foil. They will keep well for a couple of days. They also freeze beautifully. Serve as they are or with the Smoky Corn Salsa (recipe follows).

Smoky Corn Salsa
Makes about 3 cups

This is a delightful salsa that belongs to summer. Sometimes when I am buying fresh corn, I buy two extra ears just to make corn salsa. For a quick lunch, I spoon it over steamed rice or black beans. That's pure heaven in a bowl.

Remove husks and silk from corn and rinse off well. Steam for 2 minutes. Place in colander and rinse under cool water. Stand ear of corn in a bowl to cut off kernels (otherwise the kernels tend to bounce all over the kitchen). Cut the tomatoes, red onion, and red bell pepper the same size dice. Mince the jalapeños, reserving a few seeds to add back later.

Combine the corn kernels, diced tomato, onion, bell pepper, and chiles. Dress with the lime juice, olive oil, chipotles, salt, and cilantro. Sprinkle in a few of the reserved chile seeds to lend authority to your salsa. Serve as a relish with the Smoked Chicken Chipotle Tamales or put Smoky Corn Salsa over rice, beans, or pasta. This salsa is also a great accompaniment to anything barbecued.

SMOKY CORN SALSA

2 ears fresh, sweet corn (white or yellow)

2 ripe tomatoes

3/4 cup diced red onion

3/4 cup diced, cored red bell pepper

2 minced, seeded, cored jalapeño chiles

Juice of 2 limes

1 tablespoon olive oil

2 teaspoons pureed chipotle en adobo

1/2 teaspoon salt

1/4 cup minced cilantro

Chiles Rellenos from the Authentic Cafe
Serves 4

CHILES RELLENOS FROM THE

AUTHENTIC CAFE

4 crisply fresh poblano chiles

3 beaten eggs

1 tablespoon water

1 cup blue cornmeal

1 tablespoon crushed cumin
   seeds

1/2 tablespoon granulated
   garlic

1 tablespoon black pepper

2 teaspoons kosher salt

1/2 tablespoon crushed dried
   oregano

1 teaspoon New Mexican chile
   powder

1-1/2 cups grated mozzarella

1/4 cup grated smoked
   mozzarella

1/4 cup grated Gouda
   (see recipe note)

1/2 cup minced cilantro

1/8 cup minced epazote
   (optional but good)

These stuffed chiles are the best! Roger Hayot, the chef-owner of The Authentic Cafe in Los Angeles likes big flavors and chipotles.

First char chiles until surface is blackened. Place in paper bag to steam for 10 minutes. Peel off charred skin. Slit open each chile along one side. Reach in and pull out seeds which will be in a heavy cluster at top of chile.

Beat eggs with the water and set aside. Stir together the blue cornmeal, cumin, granulated garlic, pepper, salt, oregano, and chile powder. Place mixture on a piece of wax paper. Blend the cheeses, cilantro, and epazote.

If you don't have all of the cheese types, substitute with Monterey Jack or Italian fontina or just use mozzarella.

Stuff equal amounts of grated cheese into each chile. Each chile will hold about 1/2 cup cheese.

Holding the stuffed chile together at the seams, roll in the flour. Dip into the beaten egg and then roll gently in the cornmeal mixture so that the chile is well-encrusted.

While you are preparing the chiles, the oil should be heating in a heavy skillet. When oil is hot, fry one chile at a time, spooning hot oil over it. Turn chile once. Fry until chile is golden brown, about 2 minutes. Alternatively, you can place all of the chiles rellenos on an oiled baking sheet. Mist twice with olive oil or canola oil spray. Bake until golden brown in a preheated oven for 18 to 20 minutes.

Serve chili topped with Salsa Quemada (page 118).

1/2 cup all-purpose flour
1-1/2 cups canola oil for frying chiles or alternatively mist the coated chiles with canola oil spray

You can also save considerably on fat grams by using reduced-fat cheese or part-skim mozzarella cheese for the filling.

My collection of beautiful dried and smoked chiles.

Pueblito's Mole
8 servings or about 2 quarts mole sauce

When my husband and I spent almost four years in central Mexico, Pueblito worked for us in our rambling house in the hills above the large colonial city of Queretaro. She loved to cook as much as I did so we bravely plunged into *Mastering the Art of French Cooking, Volume I* by Julia Child and Simone Beck, a wedding gift from my mother-in-law.

Our Mexican friends were romanticized by anything French and so they were served experiments from "The Book." Our American friends wanted the real Mexican food and so Pueblito and I would fix her recipes for Chiles Rellenos (stuffed with Chihuahua cheese) or long-simmered mole and chicken. Mole is time-consuming but not at all difficult to make. The worst part is assembling all of the ingredients. Once you taste the mole, the task of collecting chiles and toasting everything will almost be forgotten.

Those years spent cooking French one day from "The Book" and Mexican the next day from Pueblito's repertoire are some of my fondest memories.

PUEBLITO'S MOLE

4 ancho chiles

6 mulato chiles

4 pasilla chiles

1/2 cup almonds

4 tablespoons sesame seeds
  (2 tablespoons reserved for
  garnish)

2 tablespoons pepitas (hulled
  pumpkin seeds)

1 stale tortilla

1 stale piece of French bread

4 medium tomatoes

4 cloves unpeeled garlic

Toast the chiles on a griddle or in a wide flat skillet. They should soften a little and darken in color but not burn. Break off stems and shake out most of seeds. Pour boiling water over chiles and let them soak at least 45 minutes.

While they are soaking, prepare the rest of the ingredients. One of the most important of techniques required for making classic Mexican sauces such as mole is the toasting of all the ingredients. To make this easier, I place each type of nut in a separate cake pan and the bread in a separate pan. Toast it all at once in a preheated 350° oven for about 10 minutes. Sesame seeds and almonds should be toasted to a golden brown. Allow all the nuts and seeds to cool while you prepare the tomatoes and garlic.

Turn oven up to 400°. Place tomatoes and cloves of garlic in a pan and roast for 15 minutes. Remove the cores and skins of tomatoes. Remove hulls of garlic. Set aside. Soak the raisins in hot water.

Now that the chiles are toasted and soaked, the seeds and nuts toasted, and the tomatoes roasted, you can begin grinding them up into a mole. Using a spice grinder or electric coffee mill reserved for this purpose, grind up the seeds, nuts, and spices in batches. Set aside.

Using a blender, puree the soaked chiles in four batches, adding about 3/4 cup chicken broth to each batch to facilitate grinding. To the last batch of chiles, add all of the ground seeds, nuts, spices, raisins, the tortilla, and toasted bread. Puree together. Pour half of this mixture into the bowl holding the three other batches of ground chiles. Now add the garlic and tomatoes to the blender. Puree. Stir everything together.

Note:
The ground up corn tortilla and
bread serve as thickeners for
the mole sauce.

Heat the oil in a heavy, deep 5-quart pot with a lid. Add mole sauce and cook briskly for a few minutes. Stir constantly so it does not burn. Add the salt and Mexican chocolate, which will take the rough edges off the sauce, and more broth if the mole still appears too thick.

3 tablespoons raisins

4 whole cloves

1/2 cinnamon stick

3 to 5 cups homemade chicken stock (see recipe), used to thin out mole sauce

2 tablespoons canola oil or lard if you prefer

1 teaspoon salt

1-1/2 ounces Mexican chocolate such as the Ibarra brand

2 3-pound disjointed chickens or 4 whole breasts

2 tablespoons canola oil

1 onion, sliced

2 chipotle chiles or smoked chiles

Water or chicken stock

Creations with Chipotles   109

It is best to add only a little broth at a time. Simmer mole for 45 minutes to strengthen the marriage of flavors. You can prepare the mole anywhere from 1 to 3 days in advance.

Brown the chicken parts in the oil, turning at least once. Add the sliced onion, chipotle chiles, and 3 cups of water or chicken stock. Simmer for 30 minutes. If using breasts, simmer for 20 minutes. Place the cooked chicken and the 2 chipotles into the pot of mole and cook together for at least 1 hour so the chicken parts will be imbued with the myriad of flavors. To serve, place chicken on platter and sprinkle with the reserved 2 tablespoons of toasted sesame seeds. Serve with lots of warm corn tortillas to soak up the mole, and plain rice.

If you wish an easier presentation, simply broil chicken breasts and glaze them with mole at serving time.

CHAPTER III

SALSAS WITH CHIPOTLES

Salsas are the backbone and lifeblood of Mexican cooking. I always have some homemade salsa in the refrigerator to help me make quick meals. I can be content with lovely salsa spooned over a bowl of rice or crisp romaine lettuce. Chipotles add even more complexity to simple, pure salsas.

I cannot live without salsa. Neither should you. Life is just too short.

Ernesto's Tomatillo Chipotle Salsa
Makes 3-1/2 cups

The fruitiness of Mexican tomatillos goes well with smokiness of chipotles (or moritas). They are often paired in salsas throughout Oaxaca. This particular salsa is good on its own or as a sauce for enchiladas or chiliquiles.

Soak the chipotles or moritas in boiling water for 15 to 30 minutes depending upon their dryness.

Broil or char tomato and blacken the tomatillos.

Fry the chopped onion in an ungreased frying pan (nonstick is preferable) until slightly browned but not burned. Add garlic toward the end so it doesn't burn.

Place soaked chipotles, onions, garlic, tomato, tomatillos, half of broth, salt, vinegar, the adobo, and cilantro in blender (preferable to a food processor for this salsa). Puree.

Simmer the salsa in a saucepan, adding the rest of broth. Simmer for 15 minutes. Taste for seasoning. Serve warm.

In place of homemade chicken broth, Mexican cooks often season hot water with Maggi or chicken granules. This works well for salsa.

ERNESTO'S TOMATILLO

CHIPOTLE SALSA

3 chipotles or moritas,
  depending upon the heat

l large tomato, broiled or
  charred over flame

1 pound of tomatillos,
  blackened

1 cup chopped onions

2 cloves garlic

1-1/2 cups light chicken broth
  (see recipe note)

1/2 to 1 teaspoon salt

1 teaspoon rice vinegar

3 teaspoons chipotle en adobo,
  pureed

2 tablespoons cilantro

Smoked Fire

This recipe was previously printed in my *Healthy Fiesta Cookbook* and is still one of my favorites though almost embarrassingly easy. It kind of balances out the more time-consuming salsas like the one above although if you want to make it more difficult you could use a pound of fresh plum tomatoes and char them. Would that make you feel better?

Place tomatoes, chipotle puree, and garlic in a food processor and roughly puree. This salsa will keep stored in a glass jar in the refrigerator for a couple of weeks.

Spread this salsa over a flour tortilla and cover with several thin slices of cheese. Broil in toaster oven until bubbly. Great snack!

SMOKED FIRE

1 28-ounce can plum tomatoes, drained

4 tablespoons pureed chipotles en adobo

4 minced cloves garlic

Private Reserve Salsa

Alec Diaz, a friend of my mine and the owner of Chileto's in Santa Barbara, runs a taco stand with a gourmet salsa bar. He keeps a stash of the good stuff behind the counter. This is the salsa fired up with chipotles and dearly loved by the Santa Barbara aficionados. If you ask, he'll let you have some of the Private Reserve.

Fry the onion in the oil until almost blackened. Add garlic at the end.

Place onion, garlic, grilled tomatoes, chipotles, adobo, salt, pepper, and cilantro in blender and roughly puree. Simmer salsa briefly in skillet to set flavors.

PRIVATE RESERVE SALSA

1 cup chopped onion

1 tablespoon canola oil

4 cloves minced garlic

1-1/2 pound grilled tomatoes (you can also broil them)

2 chipotles, soaked in hot water

1 tablespoon pureed chipotles en adobo

1 teaspoon salt

1/2 teaspoon black pepper

2 tablespoon minced cilantro

Alex Diaz serving tortas at his Taqueriá.

Lee James and Doña Lupe's Cayenne Salsa

Makes 3/4 cup

This is the only recipe in this book which does not contain chipotles except the chocolate desserts, but it's too good a recipe to omit and since it was given to me by Lee James who sells premier smoked chiles, I felt it was blessed by the chipotle gods anyway. Doña Lupe, Lee's helper tries to have the last word on chiles.

Pour hot water over dried tomatoes and soak for 15 to 20 minutes.

Next put roasted peppers, water, softened tomatoes, salt, and garlic in the blender and puree. This salsa is picante so it is best to lightly drizzle onto things to liven them up.

When I make up this salsa I store it in old soda pop bottles or an old catsup bottle so it is easy to drizzle its fire inside quesadillas and sandwiches.

Use your own sun dried tomatoes or send to the Just Tomatoes Company, Box 807, Westley, Ca. 95387, 209-894-5371. They produce delicious soft, slowly dried tomatoes.

LEE JAMES AND DOÑA LUPE'S CAYENNE SALSA

1/2 cup dried tomatoes, reconstituted

2 fresh cayenne peppers, roasted in pan until spotted with black flecks

1/2 cup water

1/2 teaspoon salt

1 clove garlic

Oaxacan Dishwasher's Salsa
Makes 1-1/2 cups

One morning after going to the early farmer's market in Santa Barbara, we stopped in at a diner for breakfast. The place was packed but there were two spots at the counter right near the stove. When we asked for salsa for our omelettes, the cook quietly slipped us a soup bowl of red, wicked looking salsa. After one bite, we knew it was special.

The waitress confided that we were sitting on the magic stools. When you sit there, the cook treats you like royalty. That explained our salsa. Before we left, he showed us his bin of dried chiles. He proudly gave the credit to his Oaxacan dishwasher and even told me a rough version of the recipe.

This is a jewel of a salsa with a mouthful of different flavors. It is a good example of how different each dried chile can taste. This is the kind of salsa you would expect to be served in some little cafe deep in Mexico—like in Oaxaca.

Roast the tomatoes in a 400° oven for 20 minutes.

Toast all of the chiles in a dry pan until they are softened. The arbol chiles should change to a toasty red—not blackened! Do not burn the chiles or they will be bitter.

Snip the chiles into small slivers using scissors. Shake out the seeds and reserve.

Place chile slivers in a blender along with the roasted tomato and all of its pan juices, the water, garlic, and salt. Puree into salsa.

Before serving sprinkle a teaspoon of chile seeds on top to lend authority to the salsa. Give the rest of the seeds to the birds or live dangerously and put them all in the salsa.

OAXACAN DISHWASHER'S SALSA

2 tomatoes

4 arbol chiles

2 chipotle chiles

4 cascabel chiles

1 guajillo chile (can substitute a California)

1/4 cup water

1 clove garlic

1/2 to 1 teaspoon salt

Salsa Quemada (Charred Salsa)
Makes 3 cups salsa

SALSA QUEMADA

(CHARRED SALSA)

6 tomatoes, blackened over a
   gas flame or barbecue grill

2 to 4 jalapeño chiles, blackened over grill or gas flame

1 small onion,
   cut into pieces

2 cloves garlic

1 tablespoon chipotle puree or
   substitute freshly smoked
   chipotle

1/2 teaspoon salt

Juice of 1 lime

Place blackened tomatoes, cut in half and seeded, into bowl of a food processor. Cut jalapeños in half and seed. Add chile halves to the tomatoes along with onion pieces, garlic, chipotle, salt, and lime juice. Roughly chop so there are no large pieces but there is still texture.

Simmer the salsa in a saucepan to take off the raw edge and blend the flavors.

Zucchini Salsa Stuffed into Plum Tomato Shells with Chipotle Mayonnaise
12 appetizers or 3 cups salsa

This unusual and delicious recipe of Michele Anna Jordan of the Jaded Palate in Sonoma can be taken as a whole or in parts. The zucchini salsa can be eaten as a little side or relish or stuffed into hollowed out plum tomatoes.

Michele is the author of *Oil and Vinegar* and *A Cook's Tour of Sonoma*, besides being a chipotle supporter.

If you will be using the plum tomatoes, prepare for stuffing by slicing off tops of each plum tomato. Do not halve lengthwise. Turn the shells upside down on paper towels to drain for at least 30 minutes before filling. Blot insides of shells to absorb excess moisture. Let the shells drain while you prepare the zucchini salsa.

Dice the squash by cutting lengthwise slices. Cut slices into sticks. Cut sticks into 1/4-inch dices. Stir together with the diced peppers, serrano, chipotle, and

ZUCCHINI SALSA STUFFED INTO PLUM TOMATO SHELLS WITH CHIPOTLE MAYONNAISE

12 large plum tomatoes for stuffing (optional)

1 zucchini, 1/4-inch dice, about 2/3 cup

1 yellow squash, 1/4-inch dice, about 1/2 cup

1/2 cup red bell pepper, 1/4-inch dice

1/2 cup yellow bell pepper, 1/4-inch dice

1/4 cup purple bell pepper, 1/4-inch dice

1 serrano chile, minced finely

1 smoked tam jalapeño or the smoked chile pasado, slivered, or substitute 2 teaspoons pureed chipotle en adobo

1 medium tomato, skinned, seeded, and finely minced

Juice from 1 lime

2 teaspoons olive oil

Salt and freshly ground pepper to taste

Chipotle mayonnaise (see next recipe)

Cilantro leaves for garnish

tomato. If you cannot find all the colored peppers, try to use at least red and green.

Season with the lime, olive oil, salt, and pepper. Serve as a side relish or stuff a heaping tablespoon into each drained tomato shell. Top with a teaspoon of chipotle mayonnaise and cilantro leaf.

Chipotle Mayonnaise
Makes 1 and 1/2 cups

There is nothing as velvety and unctuous as homemade mayonnaise, but if you need an alternative, blend the lemon juice, mustard, pureed chipotle, and cilantro into store-bought mayonnaise.

Place two eggs in bowl of warm water for 5 minutes; then separate yolk and white of 1 egg. Place the yolk and the whole egg into the bowl of a food processor along with lime juice, salt, and lemon juice. (Reserve the remaining egg white for another use.)

Slowly drizzle in the oil through the feed tube while the processor is running. When the mayonnaise is emulsified, add the 2 tablespoons boiling water also while the processor is running. Next add the mustard, chipotle, and cilantro. Blend for a few seconds. In place of the pureed chipotle en adobo, you may use 1 to 2 freshly smoked chipotles.

CHIPOTLE MAYONNAISE

1 whole egg

1 egg yolk

3 teaspoons lime juice

1/2 teaspoon salt

2 tablespoons lemon juice

1-1/4 cups canola oil

2 tablespoons boiling water

2 teaspoons Dijon mustard

2 tablespoons pureed chipotle en adobo

2 tablespoons cilantro

Fresh Pineapple Salsa
3 cups salsa

This salsa sings alongside grilled fish, chicken, or pork tenderloins and is a nice surprise for people that have a stuck-in-a-rut attitude about salsa.

You will need about half a pineapple. Trim off outer skin, cut out core, and dice the pineapple you will need.

Trim off one thick slice of jicama and dice.

Stir together: the pineapple, jicama, red onion, serrano chile, chipotle, rice vinegar, and cilantro.

FRESH PINEAPPLE SALSA

2 cups diced fresh
* pineapple*
1/2 cup peeled and diced
* jicama*
1/3 cup diced red onion
1 minced serrano chile
1 freshly smoked chipotle
* chile, cut into slivers with*
* scissors or 2 teaspoons*
* pureed chipotle en adobo*
1 tablespoon rice vinegar or
* pineapple vinegar*
1/4 cup snipped cilantro

Jicama is a Mexican root vegetable. Its bland, crisp texture absorbs other flavors like a sponge making it a perfect foil for the softer pineapple.

Orange and Fresh Chipotle Salsa
Makes 3 cups salsa

When I was experimenting with smoking red jalapeños, I pulled the smoked chiles out of the smoker after only 3 hours to make this salsa. The chiles were still soft and succulent and combined beautifully with the oranges.

If the oranges have a lot of white pith, remove it using a sharp paring knife. Slice oranges and then cut into small dice. Cut chipotle into small slivers using scissors. Squeeze lime juice over oranges and chipotle. Stir in onion, cilantro, salt, and sugar.

Serve as a garnish to poultry or grilled food.

ORANGE AND FRESH CHIPOTLE

SALSA

4 peeled navel oranges

1 freshly smoked red jalapeño
  or softened dried chipotle

Juice from 2 limes

1/2 cup diced red onion

2 tablespoons finely minced
  cilantro

Pinch of salt

1 teaspoon sugar.

Tropical Salsa
1 quart salsa

This salsa from my *Salsa Book* remains a favorite in my kitchen. In the summer it accompanies grilled fish and in the winter, when good tomatoes are not available, Tropical Salsa again appears but with turkey or our favorite crown pork roast Thanksgiving dinners.

First dice all of the fruits and vegetables: the pineapple, mango, papaya, persimmon, jicama, onion, red bell pepper, and serrano chile. If it is difficult to find one or two of the fruits, you can delete them but part of the charm of this recipe is the dazzling color and variety of the salsa. The Fuyo persimmon is the type that is apple-like and eaten when crisp.

Combine all of the chopped ingredients and the pomegranate seeds.

TROPICAL SALSA

1 cup fresh pineapple, peeled and diced

1 mango, peeled and diced

1 papaya, peeled, seeded, and diced

1 Fuyu persimmon, peeled and diced

1/2 cup jicama, peeled and diced

1 cup red onion, finely diced

1/2 cup red bell pepper, diced

1 serrano or jalapeño chile, seeded and minced

Red juicy seeds from 1 whole pomegranate

When I have a soft, freshly smoked chipotle, I prefer using it to the ground chipotle. Use scissors to cut thin snippets of chipotle into the salsa.

1 chipotle chile, ground to powder in spice mill or substitute fine slivers of freshly smoked chipotle

1 teaspoon sugar

1/2 teaspoon powdered ginger

Juice from 1 lime

1 tablespoon rice vinegar

Pinch of salt

3 tablespoons finely snipped cilantro

Important!
Do not use chipotle en adobo here.

Stir the sugar, powdered ginger, lime juice, rice vinegar, pinch of salt, and cilantro into the salsa. This salsa keeps well for a couple of days so you can stir it together in the morning before a dinner.

To accompany barbecued seafood, I like to serve the Tropical Salsa chilled but during the winter I serve it slightly warmed as a side to roast turkey, Cornish hens, or pork. Heat for ninety seconds on full power in a microwave or heat gently in a saucepan for just 2 minutes. You don't want to cook it, just heat it.

Freshly Smoked Roma Tomato and Chipotle Salsa
3 cups salsa

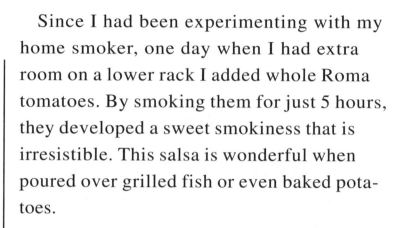

Since I had been experimenting with my home smoker, one day when I had extra room on a lower rack I added whole Roma tomatoes. By smoking them for just 5 hours, they developed a sweet smokiness that is irresistible. This salsa is wonderful when poured over grilled fish or even baked potatoes.

Dice the Roma tomatoes. Cut the two regular tomatoes in half crosswise and squeeze over the sink to remove seeds and excess juice. Dice and stir with red onion, minced chipotles, serrano, cilantro, lime, and salt.

FRESHLY SMOKED ROMA TOMATO

AND CHIPOTLE SALSA

6 smoked Roma tomatoes

2 regular tomatoes (unsmoked)

1 cup diced red onion

2 soft, freshly smoked chipotles, minced

1 serrano chile, minced

1/4 cup cilantro

Juice of 1 lime

1/2 teaspoon salt

Warm Tomatillo Chipotle Glaze for Steaks and Chicken
Makes about 1 and 3/4 cups sauce

Always keep a can of tomatillos in your pantry. They aren't as good as fresh but they're good. When you have someone show up unexpectedly, you pull out the tomatillos and chipotles en adobo. This sauce is easily put together in 10 minutes. While the chicken breasts are quickly grilling and the rice is steaming, you make the sauce. This is the kind of thing to do on a Sunday night when you want something warming but easy. As you pour the sauce over the rice and chicken (or steak), you'll feel very smart.

Sauté the onion in the olive oil until softened. Add the rest of the ingredients. Simmer a few minutes and then puree in a blender.

Place puree back into the skillet and simmer for another couple of minutes. Spoon sauce over simple grilled steaks or pounded chicken breasts.

WARM TOMATILLO CHIPOTLE GLAZE FOR STEAKS AND CHICKEN

1/2 cup chopped red onion

2 teaspoons olive oil

3 cloves minced garlic

1 cup canned tomatillos, drained or about 8 fresh tomatillos, simmered in 1 cup water for 10 minutes

2 tablespoons pureed chipotles en adobo

Rancho Mesilla Mantequilla

Rancho Mesilla is a chile ranch in New Mexico and owner, Stuart Hudson, gave me one of his favorite ways of using smoked chiles. He cool-smokes peeled red New Mexico chiles (chiles pasados) which in the end kind of resemble fruit leather. Use this pumpkin-colored butter on tortillas, baked or steamed squash, corn, or over grilled chicken filets.

Blend all of the ingredients together or place ingredients in food processor and pulse so that the texture of the pecans and pieces of chile remain.

RANCHO MESILLA MANTEQUILLA

4 ounces or 1 stick
  unsalted butter

3 cloves minced garlic

1 dried red chile (New Mexico,
  California, guajillo), toasted

1 freshly smoked chipotle or
  1 smoked chile pasado

3 tablespoons chopped, toasted
  pecans

1 tablespoon Gold Tequila
  (optional)

1 tablespoon minced cilantro

1/2 teaspoon salt

If you are using a very dry chipotle, soak it in hot water for 30 minutes before you process with the butter.

Cilantro Chipotle Pesto
Makes about 1 and 1/2 cups pesto

When you work on a cookbook, you always develop favorites. This recipe is one of those, and I always have a jar of this handy as it is good for a quick meal. Serve with pasta, corn on the cob, or spread some on thin baguette slices. Toast until bubbly.

Reconstitute chipotles by soaking in very hot water until soft and pliable. Seed chiles and cut into strips. If you are using freshly smoked chipotles, you can omit the soaking step.

It is easy to finely chop cheese in the food processor by just using the knife blade attachment. When cheese is chopped, add the chipotles, cilantro, garlic, lime juice, pepper vinegar, and olive oil. Process until you have a coarse puree.

CILANTRO CHIPOTLE PESTO

1 to 2 chipotles

3/4 cup grated Asiago cheese

1 bunch cilantro (washed, dried, and most of stems removed)

4 garlic cloves

Juice of 1 lime

1 tablespoon pepper vinegar (or use more lime juice)

1/2 cup plus 1 tablespoon flavorful olive oil

Honey Chipotle Barbecue Sauce
Makes 2/3 cup sauce

There is always a jar of this light but fiery barbecue sauce in my refrigerator, because it can be brushed over boneless chicken breasts for grilling and barbecuing. It is easy and makes the chicken special. Also good over steak or pork loin.

HONEY CHIPOTLE BARBECUE

SAUCE

4 chipotles adobado or 4
* tablespoons chipotle puree*
3 cloves garlic
1/4 cup honey
2 tablespoons brown sugar
2 tablespoons Dijon mustard
* with seeds*
1/4 cup apple cider vinegar
1/2 teaspoon cumin seeds,
* crushed*
1/2 teaspoon salt
2 tablespoons cilantro

Place chipotles, garlic cloves, honey, brown sugar, mustard with seeds, vinegar, cumin, salt, and cilantro in bowl of food processor and puree.

Easiest Fiery Barbecue Sauce in the World

Makes about 3 cups sauce

We have had huge success with this sauce so easy it's embarrassing. Use for barbecued chicken or ribs. We have even poured this over beans and people have loved it.

Stir barbecue sauce, chipotle puree, garlic, and molasses together.

Brush this sauce on the meat toward the end of cooking when it is just about done. If you brush it on early, it will burn.

Something Good!
Place 1 and 1/2-inch thick slices of yam or sweet potato brushed with oil on your grill while you are barbecuing. The sweet, smoky yams are a great accompaniment to the fiery barbecue.

EASIEST FIERY BARBECUE SAUCE IN THE WORLD

1 bottle good-brand, store-bought barbecue sauce (18 ounces)

1/2 cup pureed chipotles adobados

4 to 6 cloves garlic, minced

1/4 cup molasses (sweetness to balance the heat!)

Chipotle Paste
Makes 1 cup puree

A cook who loves chipotles should never be without this. It keeps almost indefinitely in a glass jar and makes life much easier. You can stir it into mayonnaise, sauces, marinades, or pots of soup or chili. This puree is like old reliable when you cannot find good dried chipotles. Don't you love recipes with one ingredient?

Place in food processor or blender and puree. Store in glass jar.

CHIPOTLE PASTE

1 8-ounce can chipotles en adobo

Summer in a Jar
Makes 2 quarts pickled vegetables

I came up with this recipe one morning when I had gone to Lombardi's Vegetable Stand down Bouquet Canyon near our house. It was August and the heat wave had turned the jalapeños bright red and the floral gem chiles (milder than jalapeños) bright orange. The zucchini were bright green fingers. Since one of our favorite snacks is pickled Jalapeño Carrots, I decided to pickle everything beautiful from the stand—well, almost everything.

Prepare vegetables and arrange attractively with the herbs in a 2-quart glass jar. Cut at least 5 of chiles in half before putting in the jar to make your pickled vegetables more picante. If you want your vegetables really spicy, cut all the chiles in half before putting in the jar. If you leave the chiles whole your mixture will not be picante.

Make a brine by combining the vinegars, water, salt, sugar, and garlic in a pot. Simmer for 10 minutes and then pour the hot liquid over the vegetables in the jar. Place on a lid so they will steam in the brine. Marinate several hours before using.

Serve the vegetables as appetizers or to accompany sandwiches. Slice the pickled chiles and use in salsas or over nachos. They are much better than store-bought pickled chiles.

SUMMER IN A JAR

2 bunches carrots, peeled, trimmed, and halved

4 zucchini, halved and ends trimmed

10 chiles: assortment of red and green jalapeños or other small colorful chiles

1 chipotle chile

1 sprig cilantro

1 sprig fresh oregano

4 bay leaves

2 cups apple cider vinegar

1/2 cup rice vinegar

1-1/2 cups bottled water

1-1/2 teaspoons salt

1 teaspoon sugar

3 cloves of whole garlic

Aztec Pears
8 servings

If I lived during the times of the great Aztec city of Tenochtitlan and was preparing a magnificent autumnal feast, I would roast wild guajolotes (turkeys) to accompany steamed maize cakes, and these spiced pears among the many rich platters of food. As fitting for the times, I would naturally decorate the pears with leaves of gold; but in my own modern kitchen, I am usually forced to use leaves of mint or lemon verbena.

These exotic pears will delight your guests when served during Thanksgiving or Christmas to accompany turkey, pork, or game. The pears are both sweet and picante. They are to be eaten as you would a chutney. The recipe also works well with peaches.

In blender jar combine soaked chipotle, orange juice concentrate, water, vinegar, wine, sugar, and honey. Blend. Pour into saucepan. Add canela, cloves, and whole chipotle (if you want extra heat). Simmer briskly for 15 minutes to create the syrup.

Pour the boiling syrup over the prepared fruit in a deep bowl. Steep the fruit several hours before serving. The fruit keeps well for a week. I like to warm it in the syrup before serving (but be careful not to cook it any further.) Simmer 1 cup of the syrup for 10 minutes in a shallow saucepan to create a thicker glaze to coat the fruit. This is an optional step and just makes the pears a little prettier when served.

Serve 1/2 pear or peach glazed with 1 tablespoon thickened syrup or the syrup from the marinade. Garnish with a mint leaf.

AZTEC PEARS

1 whole chipotle chile, soaked in hot water for 15 minutes

1/2 cup frozen orange juice concentrate

1 cup water

1/4 cup white vinegar

1/2 cup white wine

3/4 cup sugar

2 tablespoons honey

2 cinnamon sticks, preferably canela

4 cloves

1 whole chipotle, optional

4 ripe but firm pears or peaches, peeled and halved

Hint:
It is important to use firm but ripe fruit. If pears are too soft or overly ripe, they will become mushy when marinated in the hot syrup.

CHAPTER IV

*C*HOCOLATE

I think one should always try to achieve a certain balance in one's life, sort of the yin and the yang. Of course this philosophy applies to what you eat also. I have always loved chocolate and although I would love to have it every day, I have had to curtail this habit a little. I have chocolate every other day.

It was not surprising to make the discovery that people who love chocolate also love chiles. The famous dessert cook, Maida Heatter, the author of *The Great Chocolate Dessert Book* among her many books, admits to sharing this devotion to chiles and chocolate. Can you be convinced that one balances the other? Therefore, following a meal including chiles, especially chipotles, you have every excuse to eat some chocolate.

Included within this chapter are some recipes to help you achieve cosmic chile-chocolate balance.

Chocolate Almond French Cake
8 servings

This cake, learned twenty years ago from Simca Beck, is one of the best chocolate desserts I know how to make. It never fails to elicit cries of pleasure from those who eat it. The icing is so simple, unctuous and easy, I use it on top of many other things like my brownies, because it is like liquid truffles. The recipe below was included in my *Healthy Fiesta Cookbook*, but I could not omit it here because I love it so.

Soak the raisins in the brandy at least an hour before starting the cake. Grease a 9-inch cake pan and line with parchment. Grease the parchment with shortening or butter. Preheat oven to 375°. (The correct oven temperature is crucial to the success of this cake.)

Place chocolate and water in top of double boiler and melt over low heat. Alternatively, melt in your microwave oven. Watch and stir! Place melted chocolate in mixer bowl and, with mixer on low speed, add pieces of the soft butter.

CHOCOLATE ALMOND

FRENCH CAKE

1/4 cup raisins

1/4 cup good brandy,
* bourbon or cognac*

Parchment for cake pan

Shortening or butter to grease
* pan and parchment*

7 ounces semisweet or bitter-
* sweet chocolate*

3 tablespoons water

1/2 cup softened sweet butter

Next add egg yolks one at a time, then sugar and vanilla.

Combine flour and ground almonds. Add half the flour-almonds to the chocolate mixture, all of the brandy and raisins, and finish with the rest of the flour-almonds. Mix the cake batter just enough to blend.

Beat egg whites with the salt until soft peaks form; then slowly add the 1/3 cup sugar. Beat until stiff peaks are formed. Stir about 1/3 of the beaten whites into the chocolate batter to lighten and then fold in the rest. Do not overwork the batter.

Pour the chocolate batter into the prepared cake pan. Bake about 27 minutes. When a cake tester is placed in the middle of the cake, it should have a thin film of chocolate clinging to it. The cake will be crusty on the outside.

The cake puffs up in the oven and then while it is cooling, cracks are formed. Do not be alarmed. Push the cracks down as though you were patting it smooth. The icing will disguise any cracks.

3 eggs, separated

1/2 cup sugar

2 teaspoons vanilla

4-1/2 tablespoons cake flour

2/3 cups finely ground almonds

1/4 teaspoon salt

1/3 cup sugar to be added to egg whites

Chocolate Icing

CHOCOLATE ICING

4 ounces semisweet chocolate

1/4 cup strong coffee

4 tablespoons softened un-salted butter

Small gold leaves, purchased at a cake decorating or party store (optional)

Melt the chocolate in the coffee using a saucepan or in a microwave. Beat in butter in small amounts. Spread icing around sides and then top of cake. Arrange the gold leaves around the edge of cake.

The cake can be frozen, well-wrapped in plastic wrap, for a month. In this case don't put on the Chocolate Icing before freezing. If you are dying for chocolate some night (this is how we discovered this trick), remove the cake from the freezer and cut off a wedge. Zap it in the microwave (high power) just 20 seconds. The cake becomes soft and oozy on the inside, remaining crisp on the outside. If you are serving this to a guest, you could be civilized and sprinkle the chocolate wedge with powdered sugar.

Shattered Mocha Brownies
16 brownies

The pale, milk-chocolate colored top layer on these brownies shatters like chocolate glass as they cool, forming a great contrast to the fudgey interior. They simply cannot be compared to other brownies and they were inspired by Maida Heatter.

Preheat oven to 400°.

Melt butter and chocolate together in a saucepan or even better, in a microwave oven. Set aside while you beat the eggs, sugar, expresso powder, and vanilla for 6 minutes using an electric mixer. You must whip a lot of air into this mixture so it looks like a light meringue.

Using a whisk, blend the melted chocolate mixture into the egg-sugar mixture along with the flour and salt. Stir just until blended. Pour into a greased 9 x 9-inch pan. Bake for 26 minutes.

Cool on rack for 20 minutes. The surface will form cracks. Don't worry for this is as it should be. Then place the pan of brownies

SHATTERED MOCHA BROWNIES

1 stick butter

4 ounces semisweet chocolate

3 eggs

1-1/2 cups white sugar

2 teaspoons powdered expresso (Medaglia D'Oro is good)

2 teaspoons vanilla

3/4 cup all-purpose flour

1/4 teaspoon salt

into the refrigerator for at least 3 hours. This allows the fudgy interior to set up.

After chilling, cut into squares; very carefully remove brownies with a small spatula.

Shattered Brownies, waiting to be devoured.

Chocolate Kahlua Pie
8 servings
2 servings if your college-age sons are home

When I was young and gourmet, I would have scorned this pie. Too easy! Now, I base my food preferences on how good does it taste, how long does it take to make it and how many pieces are left at mid-night.

None of this pie is ever left at midnight.

Grind graham crackers in food processor. While machine is running, add the melted butter. Coat a 9-inch glass pie plate with a teaspoon of butter. Press chocolate crumbs into pie plate. Bake pie shell in preheated 350° oven for 10 minutes. Set aside to cool while you prepare the filling.

Place marshmallows and evaporated milk in a heavy saucepan. Heat gently while you stir until marshmallows melt. This will only take 3 to 4 minutes. Pour into bowl to cool. Add vanilla, coffee liqueur, cocoa powder, and expresso powder. Whisk to blend. Allow this mixture to cool for about 20 minutes.

Whip the cream and fold into the cooled pie filling. Pour into chocolate shell and refrigerate for at least 4 hours before serving. Thirty minutes before serving, make the Chocolate Lattice Topping.

Chocolate Lattice Topping
Melt the chocolate in the coffee in a small saucepan or even better, in the microwave oven. Stir in the butter. Using a spoon, drizzle the liquid chocolate in a lattice design on top of the pie. Chill at least 30 minutes before serving.

CHOCOLATE KAHLUA PIE

2-1/4 cup finely ground chocolate graham cracker crumbs or chocolate wafer crumbs

2 tablespoons melted butter

1 teaspoon soft butter

20 marshmallows

5 ounce can evaporated milk

2 teaspoons vanilla

2 tablespoons Kahlua coffee liqueur

1 tablespoons bitter cocoa powder

1/2 teaspoon powdered expresso

1/2 cup whipping cream

CHOCOLATE LATTICE TOPPING

2 ounces semisweet chocolate

1 tablespoon coffee

1 teaspoon butter

Chocolate Bread Pudding
8 servings

There is always room for more bread puddings, especially one layered with chocolate.

Lightly toast bread slices, arranged on a cookie sheet, in a preheated 350° oven for 10 minutes. Bread does not have to be completely dry. Tear bread into smaller pieces.

Beat eggs, sugar, vanilla, and cinnamon together; then blend in milk and cream.

Melt chocolate in microwave. Set aside.

Butter a deep baking dish and arrange a layer of bread pieces on the bottom. Pour on about 1-1/2 cups of milk mixture. Drizzle some melted chocolate across the pudding. Add the rest of the bread pieces. Pour on the rest of the milk mixture. Drizzle on remaining chocolate. Let the pudding sit for 20 minutes so the bread absorbs some of the milk.

Bake in preheated 350° oven for 30 to 35 minutes or until pudding is set. Serve warm pudding with softly whipped cream flavored with vanilla or bourbon.

If you wish to make this a lower-calorie dessert, you can substitute 1% milk in place of the whole milk and cream; use an egg substitute in place of whole egg; use a whipped cream substitute in place of whipped cream; but you must keep the chocolate.

Use leftover pan dulce from your breakfast to make bread pudding.

Explosiones de Chocolate

30 cookies

These cookies are called chocolate explosions in Mexico because the unbaked cookies are rolled in powdered sugar and crackle as they bake. They were a favorite along with the traditional wedding cookies on afternoon tea trays when I lived in Mexico.

Melt chocolate and butter together in a small saucepan or in a microwave oven. Remove and pour into a mixing bowl. Stir in the oil.

Beat eggs, sugar, and vanilla together until well-blended.

Stir melted chocolate-butter-oil mixture into egg-sugar batter.

Place a strainer over the mixing bowl so that you may easily sift in the flour, baking powder, and salt. Stir in the chocolate chips. These will create a wonderful fudginess in the middle of the cookies.

EXPLOSIONES DE CHOCOLATE

4 ounces unsweetened chocolate

1/4 cup unsalted butter

1/4 cup safflower oil

3 eggs

1-1/2 cups sugar

2 teaspoons vanilla

2 cups all-purpose flour

2 teaspoons baking powder

1/4 teaspoon salt

3/4 cup miniature chocolate chips

1 cup powdered sugar for coating

Chill the cookie dough, well-covered, at least 2 hours or 45 minutes in the freezer if you are in a hurry.

When ready to bake, form small 1-inch balls and roll them in the powdered sugar until generously coated. Bake in a preheated 375° oven for about 9 minutes. Cookies will expand in the oven and crackle on the surface. You may eat them right away or, after they cool, store in tin for 1 day or so. For longer storage, freeze.

Hint:
Do not use canola oil as it leaves a bitter after taste.

Explosiones de Chocolate served on brightly colored papel de china (Mexican tissue paper)

RESOURCES FOR CHIPOTLES
AND OTHER UNUSUAL MEXICAN AND SOUTHWESTERN
INGREDIENTS

DON ALFONSO FOODS

P.O. Box 201988Austin, Texas 78720-19881-800-456-6100

Don Alfonso Foods makes delicious chipotles en adobo packed in a glass jar and pureed chipotles en adobo immediately ready for the cook to stir into dishes. Carry tan chipotles, moras, and morita chiles and many of the other unusual chiles from Mexico including all the chiles for authentic mole. Catalog available.

SANTA FE SCHOOL OF COOKING

116 West San Francisco St.Santa Fe, New Mexico 87501 (505) 983-4511 For orders

They carry a wonderful masa harina (dehydrated masa) that I use for tortillas and tamales. The meal is stoneground in Texas and has incomparable flavor compared to supermarket brands. Also have exotic dried beans, dried chiles, and blue corn.They carry both Don Alfonso Chipotles and the new Santafire. Southwestern cooking classes available.

RANCHO MESILLA

P.O. Box 39Mesilla, New Mexico 88046 (505) 525-2266 For orders

Stuart Hudson will air freight New Mexican long green chiles grown along the fertile Rio Grande; chiles are fire-roasted and peel easily;also available are smoky chiles pasados, the dried red New Mexican chiles which are cold-smoked. Hot, sweet, and lighter smoke flavor than Mexican chipotles.

TIERRA VEGETABLE FARM

Healdsburg, California (707) 433-5666 for chile orders

Produce some of the most delicious chipotles I have ever tasted. Ranch-grown chiles are smoke-cured over orchard fruitwood and grapevine cuttings in an outdoor brick oven.

JUST TOMATOES

P.O. Box 807 Westley, California 95387 1-800-537-1985

Intensely sweet, vine-ripened tomatoes dried and packaged by this small company; great in salsas especially in the winter when only pink golf balls are available in supermarkets. Come in thin slices so they reconstitute almost immediately for use in cooking.

ROUND TOP CAFE, THE ROYERS

On the SquareRound Top, Texas 78954 1-800-8GROYERS

This family operation produces a delicious vinegar called Pepper Sauce which I use to spark salsas and salad dressings. Bottles are colorfully packed with red and green jalapeños, cilantro, onions, vinegar, spices, and probably something secret. I bought my first bottle in Macy's in San Francisco and was desperate when I ran out so I called the phone number on the bottle's label and reached Bud at the Round Top Cafe (shades of the Whistle Stop Cafe in "Fried Green Tomatoes"). He chatted up a storm and said,"Sure I'll send you more Pepper Sauce."

148

Index